Journey Toward the Sunrise

The true story of a Buddhist's search for the light of God

Chiga Taira

Chiga Taira

with Barbara Seaborn

Journey Toward the Sunrise
by Chiga Taira

Note: Some names in this book have been changed to protect individual's privacy.

ISBN 1-56043-245-4

For Worldwide Distribution
Printed in the U.S.A.

Companion Press
An Imprint of Genesis Communications, Inc.
P.O. Box 91011 • Mobile, AL 36691
(334) 607-9191 • (888) 670-PINE
Fax (334) 607-0885
Email: GenesisCom@aol.com

TABLE OF CONTENTS

PREFACE

The bright, Georgia sunshine is unusually warm for November. Color clings to the trees as though unwilling for the autumn beauty to end. Wind and sunlight play gently among the still changing leaves. I stand transfixed at my living room window, trying to absorb the loveliness.

Birds twitter, adding a living touch to this quiet afternoon. Frolicking children break the silence, too. Unknowingly, their innocent noises unleash memories of my childhood in Japan....

The world I knew as a child was lovely, too, and exciting. I loved exploring it all—flowers, woods, streams, even mud puddles. Nature never failed to satisfy my curiosity, and I discovered something new from her unlimited resources every day.

My discoveries were always too good to keep. Like a little reporter, my mouth emptied out a succession of stories to my patient family and friends. They heard what was beautiful or painful to me, what made me afraid or filled me with joy. They also heard a steady stream of questions. From sunrise to sunset, the warmth of a summer day to the wind, snow, or rain, I wanted to know the how and why of everything I saw.

Many sunrises and sunsets, rainstorms and snowfalls, have passed since those long ago days, and I am looking again for someone who will listen to what I have discovered. Neither my stories nor my questions are about mud puddles or "why is the snow white?" anymore. Though I never stopped exploring the physical world, as I grew older my search turned toward the things I couldn't see, but which I wanted desperately to understand: truth and the meaning of life, for myself as well as for the world.

Facing the typewriter this peaceful afternoon, alone with my thoughts, I am content to express my thoughts on these sheets of paper. Perhaps someone will read what I have discovered and remember similar thoughts of their own, or else they will be guided into a new dimension of thought which they haven't explored before. For one of my discoveries is that, in many ways, all people are alike. We all seek happiness, yet often encounter sorrow and pain instead. We have all felt lonely, discouraged, and of little use to the world. Sometimes we are paralyzed by our doubts and never bloom into the fullness of life we expected to enjoy. Ultimately, we don't understand how the natural world can be so beautiful if the crown jewel of creation, human life itself, wasn't designed to be equally as magnificent.

Like many, I have experienced much suffering in my life. But out of my pain eventually came joy, and the understanding I searched so long for was born. Out of my confusion came wisdom, and from loneliness burst forth love. I know now that every hurt was like the pain of birth—spiritual birth, as I emerged into a world alive with purpose and filled with reasons for me to be there.

The miracle which took place in my life was as unexpected as the morning glories which greeted me one summer morning in my childhood. How pretty they were as they sparkled in the early sun, wet with dew and slightly swaying in the fresh breeze. Their blossoms were as large as a baby's face, their colors a mixture of sky blue and deep, sunset pink, and I wondered who put them there just to surprise me.

Today these many years and discoveries later, I acknowledge that it is God whose unseen hands made the snow, the morning glories, and the autumn colors, just as it was He who fashioned every miracle along the route of my impossible journey to take me where He knew it was best for me to go. And when I arrived at my destination, I was surprised again. He had taken me exactly where I wanted to go.

In order to shorten the story, I have sometimes condensed two or three incidents into one in order to present the one thought or lesson which I learned from them. Also, to honor the will of God as I understand it from His Word, my story is written in the Spirit of Christ who came "not to condemn the world but that the world through Him might be saved" (John 3:17).

Throughout my life, and in the writing of this book, I am thankful for those who helped me on my journey. To those who willingly helped me, I am forever grateful. But there were many who didn't know they were helping me, yet they contributed important values to my life. The most precious blessings from God are the love, patience and encouragement of my family. I hope I may also be a blessing to them as we share the grace and word of God together through His Son, Jesus Christ.

Finally, this book would never have been possible without the love, care and understanding of my sister in Christ, Barbara Seaborn. She, with her writing ability and knowledge of the Scriptures, and her love for those who don't yet know the "Good News" of the Gospel, made sacrificial contributions to the book. Meeting her was one of the "miracles" of my journey, and I am thankful to the Lord for her. May she be a blessing to many as we share our lives together in Christ, our Lord, for His purpose. Barbara helped me tremendously on chapters 1-10.

FOREWORD

by Barbara Seaborn

Journey Toward the Sunrise is more than a good read. Although it is the story of Japanese-born Chiga Taira's long, agonizing journey of faith from Buddhism to Christianity, it is also a valuable tool for Christians who desire to bridge a culture and religion they don't understand in order to share their faith.

Readers will marvel at Chiga's imagery and, once she puts her life and faith into perspective, her insight. They'll enter her struggle to survive in post-war Japan, and to adjust when she marries an American soldier and leaves not only her country but a culture and faith that cry out to be retained. They'll weep with her when no one seems to understand what journey she is on, and they'll learn that the pat, memorized answers we Christians give a seeking public can sometimes do more spiritual harm than good. Eventually they'll rejoice when she leaves her dark night behind and awakens to her sunrise of joy. They may be surprised, however, when she doesn't declare Buddhism a "tool of the devil" as some suggest, but compares her former faith to the moon, the pale light which illumines the night until the sun, the greater light, ushers in the dawn.

The story's title is a composite of two Japanese proverbs explained early in the story. The first is spoken by an elderly woman who, during a period of near starvation after the war, walks miles to bring Chiga's family a much-needed bundle of rice. The woman declines the family's invitation to stay the night because, "Night travelers have no fear of the sunset, only the expectation of the sunrise." Later, when Chiga has just turned 15, her mother sends her away to care for a crippled relative because, she believes, "If you love your child, send him on a journey." Chiga's constant symbolism is perhaps most apparent in the recurring reference to her father's story about two frogs—the king frog who stays in his own pond and declares himself king, and the fool frog (Chiga) who travels the countryside searching for "the King of the whole world."

Chiga Taira and I were children at the same time, on opposite sides of the world while our countries fought each other in World War II. Forty years later our husbands were both soldiers in the American Army, and we were friends. Though I marvel at the unlikely circumstances which brought us together, I am deeply touched by what our meeting has done for my faith. I may have been part of the Christian fold and tended by the Good Shepherd all my life, but I doubt I really understood what Jesus meant by those "other sheep that are not of this fold" (John 10:16), until I met Chiga. I have become a stronger Christian by looking at Jesus through the eyes of that "other sheep."

I'm happy to have helped write Chiga's story so others may benefit from her journey, too. For Christians, may these words provide strength and a new desire to share the Gospel with people from every background and nationality, no matter how different from their own. For those still traveling dark, nighttime lives, may you be encouraged by Chiga's journey to press on to your own sunrise which most certainly follows the night.

Chapter One
SPRING

"Has something unusual happened to you, perhaps yesterday, last week—today?"

As I recall that day from my fading memory, I was in trouble. My grade school teacher had asked us to write a poem, but even with her suggestions, I had no idea what to write about. My classmates were all busily scribbling something on their paper, but I couldn't think of a thing to say.

In panic I glanced outside the classroom windows. When I saw the snow, falling silently from a thick, gray sky, I knew what I would write about. What had happened to me that morning on the way to school was very unusual to me. Perhaps I could turn that experience into the assigned poem....

Though I lived barely half a mile from the school, walking there through six inches of new snow without falling into the deep, watershed ditches on both sides of the road made the distance seem much longer. The wind swirled sharp bits of snow against my face as I struggled with each step. With my eyes half closed, I forced myself to follow the footsteps someone else had left behind.

My grandmother had bundled me with an extra sweater under my coat, but I still felt cold. My knapsack scraped uncomfortably against my back, and my feet were icy cold as the wetness crept inside my boots. I wanted to turn around and go home.

1

"Come on! Hurry!"

Poor visibility, or my preoccupation with myself, had kept me from noticing anyone else on the road. About ten yards in front of me, three older girls waited for me to catch up with them. They were bundled in heavy coats, too, and wore colorful mufflers on their heads. The girls sounded cheerful, but I hesitated because they were so big and I didn't know who they were, and because the snow was penetrating my face like tiny bullets and I didn't want to move. I was trying not to cry.

To my surprise, the girls ran back toward me and began to help me walk. One stood beside me and held my hand while the other two walked in front of me to shield me from the wind and snow. Listening to their laughter and conversation, I felt warm and secure. I walked tall and big, just like them.

As we approached our school gate, the wind seemed to calm and the snow to become as soft and gentle as flower petals. I felt like laughing, too, as I entered the corridor leading to my classroom escorted by my new friends.

I don't remember now what words I used to describe this incident, but my poem was judged the best in the class. I do remember my teacher saying something about my unusual awareness of the world around me. It was the first time I was able to communicate through writing. Before I had seen only in pictures, now I could "see" in words.

I enjoyed playing with my two brothers and the other children in the neighborhood, but when I was alone I would spend hours lying on the hillside or in the middle of a clover field watching cotton-like clouds float by in living pictures across the cobalt sky. What a beautiful sky it was! I wished I could touch it, feel it with my hands.

With farming so common around our village, I was also interested in the daily activities of the farmers. I already knew they worked from early morning until late in the day, but I wanted to know how they planted their seed, how they sorted the weeds from the good plants, and how they harvested their crops when the season changed.

The farmers all lived in houses built along the side and foot of a mountain slope which had been cleverly developed into terraced fields. Our rented house was there, too, facing south where we could overlook the hills and fields that stretched as far as the Aki River, which flowed east and eventually into the Pacific Ocean. Beyond the river were other fields, other mountains standing majestically against my treasured, southern sky.

One early spring day I took the narrow path leading to the fields behind our house and began my daily walk. The air was cold, but the bright sun warmed my face. As I climbed the steady hill, I came upon one of our neighbor women working alone in her field. Though she was surprised to see me, a welcoming smile spread quickly across her weathered face. To protect herself from the wind, she had covered her head and cheeks with an old towel—*Nihon-tenugui*—and tied it under her chin. She wore a dark blue, Kimono-styled short top and tight-bottomed slacks—*Monpe*—along with special working shoes—*Jikatabi*—a familiar outfit for farm women in that part of Japan.

I was puzzled by her strange-looking activity. Breathlessly, she was stamping down plant after plant, row after row, of nearly three-inch-high barley, completely crushing them it seemed to me. She moved with a light, steady rhythm, as she held both hands comfortably together behind her back. She greeted me lovingly without stopping her work.

"Is it time for your leisurely walk?" she asked.

Did she wish she were not so consumed with her toil and could walk with me? Wrinkles appeared at the corners of her round, small eyes. Oh, she was teasing me. I laughed. She always called my curious, aimless pastime the leisurely walk. She was not a beautiful woman, but very kind and cheerful. Her round, chubby face was always tanned. Her work appeared to be a source of joy.

"Why are you destroying your barley plants?" I asked in disbelief. She wiped her nose with a corner of her towel and explained:

"If we press down the barley when it is young, the roots get stronger and the plants yield better quality grain at harvest time."

"Are you sure you aren't damaging them?" I had to be sure before I offered to help her. In her high-pitched voice she continued:

"No, I am not damaging them at all. You will see. These little plants are like children who must go to school and take tests, learning from their elders and sometimes needing correction in order to become wiser in the end."

Convinced that she knew what she was doing, I walked toward her and began stamping down the barley just like she did. I even held my hands neatly behind my back like hers. My nose and cheeks soon became as red as hers, too.

I have never forgotten this incident. Years later I would understand that, just as the woman had said, stamping down those tender plants was not harmful at all, and what sometimes seemed like cruelty to a young child was necessary for my strong growth as well.

Living among farmers I learned much about their busy but unsophisticated way of life. During my so-called leisurely walks I often found myself doing the things they did—harvesting young green tea leaves with their children, gathering dried straw from their fields, cutting hay at the mountain side far away from home, or planting young rice plants in the mud field during a soft rain. Everything concerned with growing things was exciting to me, especially when I could work together with someone else.

My father, who was a teacher, was especially perceptive about my thirst for knowledge. One day when he went into the city, he brought back some beautiful books for me. Some were about the clouds, the sun, the moon and stars, and, for variety, the wonderful stories of Hans Christian Anderson. I can still remember how happy the colorful pictures and stories made me feel.

With the addition of books to my life, I fell easily and often into deep thought. Like the clouds which came from nowhere as they streamed across the sky, thoughts would enter my mind and then go away as I watched helplessly, unable to keep them long enough to learn why they had appeared in the first place. Who am I? Why am I alive? What is my purpose for being here?

Although I knew my name, whose daughter I was, and where I lived, I continued to ask those questions throughout my childhood and youth. I didn't realize it then, but a search for my spiritual identity was slowly awakening in me, like buds and leaves in the springtime—my springtime.

At some point I heard the word, "God," for the first time, and then I had new questions. What is God? Is God a person? In my logic, if there is a word, there must be something for that word to represent—like girls, snow, milk, farmers, etc. Where there were things, there had to be names for them. Yet with the word, "God," there was nothing for my mind to focus on. The meaning was completely empty to me. But though there was no content to fit the word, "God," in my mind, I still couldn't throw the word away. There had to be a "something" that was God, because there was a word, "God."

This was a puzzle at times so perplexing to me that I tried to push the thought of God out of my mind altogether. But just when I thought I had completely forgotten this and other questions, they reappeared, following me like my shadow or an unseen force that taunted me into wondering about them again and again. The memory of the farmer's wife stamping down the barley came often to my mind and I thought I must be like those young plants, except that I didn't seem to be growing at all. It was painful to discover that I really didn't know very much about anything, and I was very dissatisfied with that feeling.

I did grow, however, from a talkative, little girl into a quiet, older child in a world that was changing from peaceful to troubled times. I began to sense fear as people's faces darkened around me. A cloud of tragedy was throwing its cold shadow across one corner of my mind as if a merciless storm were approaching a peaceful town, threatening to shatter the bright rays of the sun above as it passed by. I still took my aimless walks in the woods, to the fields, and by the river, but it was different now. The very things which once filled me with great interest could not delight me anymore. I felt lonely again, even when I could hear familiar sounds like dogs barking in the distance, cows mooing inside neighborhood barns, and birds singing from nearby trees.

I couldn't wipe the fear from my mind, nor shake the loneliness that clung to me wherever I went or whatever I did. There was no way back to those innocent, happy days of my childhood. An unseen force at the bottom of my being urged me forward, but I still didn't know where I should go or what I should aim for. My aimless walks had become an aimless life.

I only knew I had to move on, define that goal, and find it. I didn't know when this transition would take place, nor what caused me to think this way, but I knew someday I would go beyond the present boundaries of my life. The will to search for that unknown something was taking deep root beneath the cold shadows of war.

Chapter 2
SIGNPOSTS

Freedom! Democracy! Peace at last!

I was eleven when World War II with its unspeakable pain and anguish finally came to a close. Like spring following a cold, dark winter, sighs of relief and joy replaced the fear that had been part of our lives during those tense four years. Now it was time to rebuild.

We greeted our new world with expectancy and great hope. New music replaced war songs. New books and movies, new clothing and food appealed to the heightened senses of those who had been deprived of so much for so long. Shoddy roadside stands, boasting everything from trinkets to necessities, sprang up on street corners all over the ruined cities.

But these new businesses were not all good, and a new kind of terror began to creep across the land. Changes were taking place too fast. People did anything for money, anything to regain their losses and buy enough rice or power to survive. Crime flourished.

While newspapers and magazines made headlines reporting the decline in moral behavior, new religions urged followers to resist this different kind of decay which was now making rubble of people's hearts as war had done to their streets.

By the time I turned thirteen I was aware of this paradox, but I couldn't understand it. The outward war may have ended, but it was the beginning of my own personal war within, a deep conflict over right and wrong. I was dissatisfied with the changes going on around me, but I lacked the wisdom or power to stop them. We needed rice, too—our monthly ration was never enough—but I didn't want to get it illegally. My heart was heavier now than it had been during the war.

It was also a time of distrust. A smile was nearly always suspect. Our friends and relatives, who could be relied upon forever, became precious possessions, but we just expected other people to cheat us, lie, or break the law in order to save their own lives or protect their families. The practice was common: outsmart others before they deceive you. In many cases bribes became the passport for official matters. In despair, some people committed suicide. To me, the price of the war had been too high. Was this freedom?

I longed for my grandmother who had died a year after the war ended. The daughter of a Buddhist priest, she often told me of spiritual things, like death and then judgment for what you did during your lifetime, and about heaven and hell. In heaven, the reward for choosing a good life, she said, you can rest in peace and joy without pain or sickness of any kind, but in hell there is suffering and much pain because of what you did wrong.

"Always be aware of *Enma* (the beautiful devil)," she warned, "because he's the one who sends you to hell."

Once, when I was about four years old, she took me to a place where there were scenes of hell painted on the walls. It was a scary experience which I never forgot. In one scene I saw people engulfed in a lake of fire, and in another there were figures walking along a rough road carrying heavy bags on their drooping backs, and expressions of hopelessness on their bony faces.

"Don't tell lies," she said. "Forgive those who wrong you no matter what the offense, and be kind to everyone—

even strangers. Be thankful for everything you have, and don't walk in the way of the serpent."

I didn't understand then what she meant by those other worlds we would live in someday, nor the meaning of the serpent, but now, as I observed the great changes in behavior all around me, her words returned to me vividly. I thought about them all the time.

Before my grandmother died, she often reminded me that she would go to heaven ahead of me and wait for me there. She was kind and gentle, and I was certain she was there now. I didn't like being left behind amid all the suffering, but I didn't ever want to die just to go to heaven. Instead, I wanted to bring heaven down to earth. I was happy for my grandmother and others who had died because they didn't have to go through this time of struggle. But, oh, how I wanted people who were sick and sorrowful to be able to live in that sweet peacefulness my grandmother had described, and to which she had gone.

My family all believed in life after death and the judgment, and they all hoped to go to heaven someday. But we had to eat and I didn't see how we could survive this postwar time without telling some lies and breaking some laws. I wanted so much to find a way to meet our needs without committing crimes or wronging anyone else, but I was only a child. I saw myself as a tiny leaf floating away in a stream. I couldn't go against the current of world change—no one could—but I felt an urgency to warn the world that we were all heading for hell together!

My mother must have felt the same inner conflict, but she was wiser than I. She often said, "Don't judge the world in such a time as this. With your limited knowledge you must not jump to conclusions about the actions of other people. Just believe that there are always eyes to see the truth somewhere. Practice looking at the root of things, not only at what they seem on the surface."

She reminded my brothers and me of our father who had died a year before the war ended, about our grandparents and the episodes in their lives that delighted us, and that the spirits of those loved ones who have died will come back to comfort us with their presence. I didn't understand this idea, either, but at least I knew their words and memories came often to me. My mother seemed at peace. Sometimes when she spoke, my troubled thoughts were peaceful, too:

"We have lost nearly everything but we still have our books and kimonos to sell or exchange for food. You can continue your education without worry, and someday you will stand on your own feet somewhere in the world. You can't depend on others to do everything for you, nor should you blame the world for what you do not have. You have the ability to do anything you want with your life by yourself." She was preparing my brothers and me for our unknown future.

Like my father, Mother was an educator, too, and a friend of many. She talked endlessly with our uneducated neighbors, helping them adjust their thinking to the new world situation. She dealt with superstitions that gripped their minds and crippled their initiative. She was buoyant. Even though our ration of rice was small, she never lost her song or her ability to spread cheer to those who knew her. She taught us not to worry about tomorrow's food, for somehow, just in time, we always had enough to eat and something to share.

Late one evening, while we were reading after our simple supper, we heard a light knock on our tightly closed door.

"Who could that be at this hour?" my mother murmured. Normally, guests didn't call after the evening meal, especially when they weren't expected. "It must be one of our neighbors," she answered herself.

"Who is there?" she called cautiously.

"Please open the door. It's me...," a soft, feminine voice replied.

With a puzzled look on her face, my mother opened the door. There in the light from our living room stood an old woman bent over nearly double because of something she was carrying on her back.

"Oh, Grandma Shigeta!" my mother cried, helping the burdened woman inside and setting her load on the dirt floor in the entrance way.

Grandma Shigeta stretched her back and stood silently for a moment as if to catch her breath. Then, placing her shoes—*zori*—neatly at the entrance to the living room, she walked quietly toward the large cushion in the middle of our tatami floor. My mother gestured for her to sit down.

When I brought hot, green tea for them both, Mother and her guest were still greeting each other in our typical Japanese custom, and exchanging news of each other's families. Grandma Shigeta's eyes caught mine as I sat down next to my mother, and I remembered.

"How big you have grown," she said to me. "I didn't recognize you at first. You were still so small when you and your grandmother used to visit me."

It had been a long time, but whenever we went to her house she greeted us with those same eyes. Even then I thought she must be a very lonely woman. I smiled now, swallowing my tears as I remembered those visits in her house, knowing my grandmother was not here anymore to greet her with me.

Finally Grandma Shigeta explained the reason for her visit at this late hour:

"I have heard that the people here are having difficulty getting enough rice, and I especially thought of you," she said thoughtfully through tearful eyes. I remembered she always had tears in her eyes.

"Yes, it's very hard," my mother replied, "but we are not

the only ones with shortages. Some people are in far worse circumstances than we are. Some families in the city have even committed suicide together. We can be thankful that we are sitting here in this room tonight, and that we are still alive."

"True, true indeed," Grandma Shigeta echoed. "You understand a farmer's life—always something to be done but we always have something to eat and share." She paused, waiting for my mother to speak again and, perhaps, to ease the burden she carried in her heart.

"Oh, yes, I understand well, but please don't trouble yourself with us. We are living in a time when we can't always have what we want," my mother said, trying to comfort the older woman, even as she acknowledged our visitor had come to comfort us.

"I couldn't sleep well thinking of your family," Grandma Shigeta continued, "and I decided to come and see how you were. The police are watching carefully to see what is happening to our rice, so I waited until sundown to make my journey. I'm sorry I couldn't carry more," she said, gesturing toward the bundle by the door, "but it is new rice and I think you will find it tastes very good."

She smiled again with her teary eyes, and took another sip from her tea cup. I glanced sideways at my mother, noticing the serious expression on her profiled face. Her eyes were on her tea cup, not on Grandma Shigeta's face. There was a long pause. Finally, Mother brushed her high bony nose with her hand, sniffed softly, and broke the silence:

"I don't know how to thank you," she said. "I know it wasn't easy for you to walk here tonight with fifty pounds of rice on your back. I'm glad you arrived safely. You must be very tired. Please eat something and spend the night with us."

While she coaxed Grandma Shigeta to stay, my mother stood up quickly to prepare food for her. I was worried, because I knew there was nothing in the house to eat. I wondered what she was going to come up with this time, my miracle mother.

Grandma Shigeta knew how empty our cupboards were. "Please sit down," she said. "I am not hungry, but I would like another cup of tea before I leave. It was nice to see you and your daughter. I'm happy now because I have done something I wanted to do for many days."

She smiled, motioned for my mother to sit down, and continued. "I must go home tonight. It's easier to walk at night than in the hot sun. As we say, night travelers have no fear of the sunset, only the expectation of the sunrise. I may be old, but my legs are strong. I will be home long before sunrise."

Grandma Shigeta lived at least four miles from our house, high in the northern part of the mountains. There were a few villages along the way, but the most beautiful of all was that one I remembered well on the high hillside where the road ended, and where this loving lady lived.

She stayed another hour, chatting with my mother and sharing memories that I knew nothing about. It made me happy to see the joy in their hearts spilling onto their faces as they talked.

Around midnight, and after a courteous, lengthy farewell, Grandma Shigeta disappeared into the chilly but clear October night. The light from the soft, white moon and stars would guide her way and lead her home. I was glad she didn't have the burden on her back anymore. Perhaps, after her visit, the one in her heart was lighter, too.

My thoughts lingered with Grandma Shigeta even after I went to bed. I could still see her tearful eyes, the tanned wrinkled face, the way her gray hair circled in a knot at the back of her head and the comb which held it neatly in place, her slightly bent back, and the dark-colored Kimono she wore. Everything about her reminded me of my grandmother and I missed her....

13

It was summer when I walked with my grandmother to the upper village to visit her former neighbors. As we progressed along the dusty, well-traveled road, I was surprised to find occasional stone markers with my grandfather's name engraved on them.

"Grandma," I asked, "why is my grandpa's name written on these posts?"

"Because your grandpa built this road, and trucks and buses could come to the upper village for the first time," she explained, looking at me with her gentle, remembering eyes. "The people in the village placed these markers along the road to honor his work."

I hardly knew him because I was only three when he died, but I did remember that I loved to sit on his lap. As I grew older, I also loved to listen to people talk about my famous grandfather. I discovered that he built our elementary school auditorium, too, and that, although he was a wealthy landlord by small town standards, he spent most of his money on the poor or in developing his village. Some misunderstood his generosity, saying he was a fool. Others called him a great man.

I would eventually learn that my grandfather was like most people—a mixture of virtue and vice. He was known to drink excessive amounts of rice wine, which some said was where his money really went, but though he was often cheated by his own workmen or his so-called friends, he never accused them of their wrongs or stopped calling them friends. By the time of his death at the age of 63, very little remained of his estate. Even those items were either given to the Temple or sold at an auction on the front lawn of what had once been his home.

I didn't care what people said. I knew I would have loved him anyway, and I knew he loved me because he left road signs here and there for me, too, so I would recognize him and be able to claim him as part of me.

The first rays of the morning sun were appearing in the eastern sky before I fell asleep against my pillow. The sunrise reminded me of Grandma Shigeta, and I hoped she had arrived home safely by now.

Bright sunlight reflected against the Shoji screen near my bed when I awoke. Though it was nearly noontime, the house was still silent.

Again my thoughts turned to my grandfather, and I wondered what he would think of this confused world if he were still alive. What advice would he have for me? Did he have a wisdom greater than that of most wealthy people? Did he know that if he left his money to family or friends it would have been used for unworthy causes or in some way soil our lives? Did he dispose of everything before his death so we wouldn't be chained as he was by our possessions? Did he give us far more than wealth when he delivered us from the responsibility of remaining on his land to care for what he had left behind?

I realized even in those youthful years that he had given me something far greater than wealth. By his example I learned that what we have does not make us what we are, and what we are will ultimately be tested when we have nothing. The satisfaction of work well done and beneficial to others, he seemed to say, was of infinitely greater value than all the wealth one incidentally earns in the process. I had confidence in his love for me, and I couldn't believe he didn't leave me anything except those markers of his work. He must have had a reason to lose everything.... To gain something? If so, I wondered, what could it be?

Now, without possessions, whether earned or inherited, I was free to go—anywhere; free to do—anything I wanted to do. In my imagination—more real than fantasy after years of practice—I thanked my grandfather for my freedom, and decided I would find out what it was that was so important to him. There had to be something behind his mysterious way of life. As my grandmother often said to me, "Your grandpa had eyes to see beyond these mountains." What did she mean? Did he see something in his future, beyond his generation to mine?

I didn't know where I would go or exactly what my future would be, but with the signposts my grandfather and others had left for me, mine wouldn't be an aimless walk any longer. Perhaps one day I would find a way to reverse the direction of the world, to point it toward heaven where there is no pain or suffering anymore. Even if I did not find the solution to this problem, I would never be able to avoid the search for it. I would never be happy seeing others suffer and heading toward that awful hell, and to do nothing meant I would go to that hell, too. I knew I might not succeed, but at least I would be pleasing those who had taught me, and there was the exciting possibility that I would reach my goal.

This was an enormous task, more than most people would consider in a lifetime, let alone attempt to solve, and I knew that I didn't make the world the way it was when I was born into it. But the example of my grandparents was too strong for me not to try something to make the world better than it was when I found it.

"Don't ask 'who did it?'" my grandmother once said. "If you see trash lying around, it's your responsibility to clean it up. That's what your eyes are for." Her words which had taken root in my life so long ago, were now beginning to bear fruit.

But how was I to begin? How would I know what makes people commit wrong? What causes one person to hurt another? What is the reason for war? Where does crime come from? Do people find happiness by hurting others, by fighting a war just because they might win? Question followed question, and my mind devoured them like a pool of quicksand.

Finally I cried out against the perpetual motion in my head. If only I knew more about people, but I was still a child. But there was one recurring thought, a silent voice that seemed to keep saying, "Learn about people from people."

Learn about people from people? Such a simple statement, but it felt right and I was momentarily satisfied by the possible solution to my problem. Now, loaded with youthful zeal, I would challenge the world with my cause. My heart became filled with hope, and I felt wise—not like my grandfather, or even my mother, but wiser than I had ever been before.

Yes, my aimless, leisurely walks were definitely over. Now I would follow the current of the world, but I would have my mind, heart, ears, and understanding open. I would learn about everyone who came into my life, even if they only passed by me briefly. I wouldn't miss anything because every tiny action could be important.

I willingly received the gift of nothing from my grandfather, and there the journey of my life began. After all, isn't zero always the beginning of everything? My heart was light as I took the first step into the future of my life.

It felt like my grandfather was taking the journey with me.

Chapter 3
THE WORLD

"If you love your child, send him on a journey."

My mother strongly believed this Japanese proverb. One day, because of her love for me and for those in need, and because I accepted a challenge I didn't understand fully at the time, I would believe it, too.

"She's not that old—about sixty, I hear—but her rheumatism is so bad she can hardly move around anymore by herself. Her nephew has been caring for her, but he's leaving soon to continue his studies in Tokyo. It'll be a good experience for you."

My mother was sending me to Beppu City, four hours away by train, to live with one of her distant relatives. I was surprised and more than a little frightened by her sudden decision, even though I knew she wasn't being unkind to me. She had faith that I would finish my schooling, care for our relative, and mature in the process. I was barely fifteen.

"You know how much others have helped us. Now it's our turn," my mother explained, pleased at my willingness to go. "Only by sharing kindness and responsibility can everyone's needs be met."

I wouldn't be completely alone in my new surroundings. My brother, Masayuki, lived in Beppu City, too, in a room he rented from our mother's widowed cousin. "Aunty," as we called her, had brought the other woman's needs to our attention.

A dead calm settled over me as I considered the changes taking place in my life. How much I had wanted to leave home, to begin my pilgrimage toward the answers I was seeking. But when it came time to go, I wasn't excited at all. Only in my imagination had such a journey been a happy idea. Now, as I prepared to begin that journey, I didn't want to give up my familiar surroundings, especially my school and my friends. I was also more afraid than I wanted to admit. Still I knew I had to go—not just because of my mother's persuasion, but because I couldn't begin my journey without leaving home.

So, with my heart emptied of its good-byes and my sparse belongings packed into an assortment of unmatched cloth bags, I prepared to leave. Realizing that I was more child than young woman, my wise mother made the journey with me.

How noisy the city seemed to me as we stepped from the train station that late March afternoon. Crowds of people scurried in all directions at once, walking or riding on every kind of transportation imaginable—rickshas, trains, three-wheeled trucks, and hordes of bicycles racing between pedestrians as if their deadlines had already passed. Songs blared from loudspeakers, symbolically urging the city to move even faster. Smells from a nearby restaurant made my stomach growl.

Some, like us, walked more slowly: tourists examining souvenir stands, neatly uniformed American soldiers walking happily with their friends, and students in sailor uniforms passing by as confidently as if they owned the street.

Beppu City wasn't one of Japan's larger cities, but it was famous for its beauty and abundant hot springs. To the East, Beppu Bay opened its gates to a stream of tourists every year. The city with its many resort hotels, surrounded the bay and sloped toward lush, green highlands. Mountain ranges peaked in the background as if to wall out all that could harm the city's loveliness. Beppu City had been spared during the war, though other cities nearby were almost totally destroyed. I thought I had never seen a sight more beautiful.

"They look about your age," my mother remarked of the students. She understood her fearful daughter, and I was glad she knew my bravery was little more than an act. I thought she looked pretty wearing her favorite striped kimono and walking fast just like a city person. Her lightly made-up face reflected the excitement of the city, and her thin, wide lips wore their usual smile as she talked.

"Yes, I know," I answered softly, wondering if the city girls would accept me as their friend. Anyone could tell at first glance that I was a country girl. No one else had deeply tanned skin or long, braided hair. Their faces were smooth and white, and their fluffy, short hair curled about their shoulders. But I determined that first day not to be afraid of the city or its people, or by my new school, or the doubts which darted in and out of my mind like the people hurrying around me now on my new city's street.

"My goodness! You've grown to be a young lady already. When you were a baby I had to carry you on my back. Do you remember?"

My brother was happy to see me, and I rejoiced at our few days together. He was more handsome than I remembered, and I was proud to walk along the street with him. He took me to restaurants and movies, and helped me become familiar with the city. Mother had returned home the day after we arrived, but Masayuki seemed happy to continue the weaning process she had so effectively begun.

He looked like he belonged in the city with his fashionable outfits, especially his plaid sports coat and dark blue slacks, but I liked him most when he looked at me with the unmistakable eyes of country folks. He worked as a translator at the American Red Cross, which sounded like a very important position. Our time together before I started school and caring for our sick relative seemed like a vacation.

During those wonderful, brief days, I thought back to our childhood when Masayuki still lived at home with us. His friends often filled our home, and whenever they went to another town for a festival or some other special occasion, they took me with them. As the youngest child and only girl in the family, I had felt protected and loved. Now I loved him back and hardly felt any fear at all in my new surroundings as he cared for me again.

Too soon Aunty took me to my new home and registered me for school. As I had been told, Hosoda Obachan (*Obachan*, similar to "aunt" in English, is an affectionate Japanese term for a distant relative or close friend) was small and sickly, but her face bore a noble expression. She had small eyes set in a round, wrinkled face, and eyebrows that gave an impression of strength. Thick lips framed her narrow mouth; her voice was unmistakably tender. I could tell she was a person of great warmth, and I liked her from the start. I would do my best to make her comfortable and happy.

"Please sit down," she said. "My nephew isn't here right now, but he'll be home soon and then we can have tea."

Hosoda Obachan moved her fragile arms and pointed to the floor cushions near the bed where she sat propped on cushions of her own. Her fingers and arms were ugly and deformed, and every movement seemed to cause her great pain.

"Yes, yes. Please don't worry about tea," Aunty said rapidly. "If you don't mind, Chiga is ready to stay here tonight.

21

She barely passed her test for the English major today."

Aunty sat on one of the cushions while I tried to hide my embarrassment and sit gracefully beside her on the other.

"Is that right?" Hosoda Obachan replied. "Well, you'll study and catch up before you know it. Perhaps your brother can help you. My nephew is studying oil painting so he wouldn't be much help to you in English."

Hosoda Obachan's words, like her movements, were slow, but I felt her compassion for me.

Aunty kept glancing at me and insisting that I could have done better if my mind hadn't been so full of excitement about the city.

"She'll do fine when she's used to her new surroundings, and she doesn't act nervous about every little thing," Aunty laughed.

"Of course; that's what it is," Hosoda Obachan smiled.

"Chiga was brought up in the country and mainly around boys, you know, so she needs to learn how to act like a lady. Please teach her some manners, and perhaps something about flower arranging, like other girls."

Aunty seemed to feel it was her duty to explain my deficiencies, and prescribe solutions for all my ignorant ways.

"Oh, we'll work together just fine," Hosoda Obachan said, seeing something in me that had obviously escaped my aunt's microscopic scrutiny. "There's a flower arranging class this Saturday which she can attend. Some of the other girls are just beginning, too.

"I want to thank you for bringing this fine girl to help me," she said further, bowing her head and becoming solemn. "My nephew will be here another month, and she can learn all about my special needs from him. I'm very glad she has come."

"Oh, don't mention it," Aunty said, bowing toward her

as we prepared to leave. "Everyone needs help these days and I'm glad I could find someone to help you. Her brother will bring her back later tonight with her things."

As we were leaving, a young man wearing a thick, gray sweater appeared at the door. He was taller and fairer-skinned than most Japanese men, but his dark, wavy hair, high noble nose, manly eyebrows, and wide smooth fore-head—plus a prominent dimple on his chin—made him very attractive. When he came nearer we could smell oil paint.

"*Konnichi-Wa!*" he greeted us with a cheerful, low voice. His large eyes were like those of my beloved country folks, and I felt I had known him for a long time.

"Oh, Hiroshi-San," Aunty said hurriedly, "I'm glad you have come. This is your replacement. We're going for her things now, but we'll be back tonight and the two of you can talk then."

"I know," he nodded. As he closed the door behind us, I felt his sympathy at the way I was being rushed along a lit-tle too soon—not just today, nor to my brother's house and back—but into the world of adulthood and grown-up responsibility. It must have been obvious that I was anything but grown up now.

Aunty hadn't meant to make me feel bad, I reasoned. It was just her way. Still, my pride was hurt and I tried all the way back to her house to rid myself of embarrassment. I knew she was trying to make Hosoda Obachan feel needed, too. But would this woman or her handsome nephew ever have confi-dence in me? If I hadn't known how desperate they were and how much they needed me, I might have been afraid they wouldn't want me to come. Perhaps they had no choice. Like all other post-war people in our country, they would make do.

"They are wonderful people, aren't they?" I forced myself to say without bitterness.

"Yes, and you can learn many things from them," Aunty answered. "Hosoda Obachan used to teach girls from Tokyo's high society. She taught them good manners, showed them how to walk with elegance or serve in the most formal tea ceremonies, and helped them create exquisite flower arrangements. She may seem poor and sickly now, but try to think of her as she was. You'll be kinder to her that way, and benefit far more from her influence on you."

As I listened to Aunty defend her harsh treatment of me, my mother's teaching came back to me: "Don't judge the world by your understanding, or your limited experience....don't look at the surface, but at the root...."

I was glad for my mother. Even though she was far away, thoughts of her comforted me now.

After a month of training, and observing how Hiroshi cared for his aunt, I was confident I could make Hosoda Obachan happy. She was very sensitive and responded gratefully to everything we did to please her. She loved the conversation of young people, of Hiroshi and his friends, and even my backward attempts to sound entertaining and wise. She was a good listener, and a good advisor to those who came to visit her. She was also a good teacher. I thought her class in flower arranging was the most exciting thing I had ever done. Best of all, she seemed pleased with me, both with my ability at home and my progress in school.

When it was time to say good-bye to Hiroshi, we wished him well in his new life in Tokyo, and, without too much anxiety, I assumed his role. I continued all the tasks he had done plus I added some of my own to please her.

The next spring I cleared our small backyard of rubbish and planted several rows of asters. When the weather warmed, I would seat her on her cushion and pull her into

24

the corridor outside our Shoji screen so she could watch me hang laundry or work in the garden. Weeks later, sparkling in the early summer sun, our flowers burst into bouquets of profuse, mixed colors. Hosoda Obachan wiped her eyes and cheeks until they were red, and told all her visitors about the flower garden and the lovely, young girl who had planted it for her. My early life among farmers had had some usefulness in the city after all. Gradually, with constant encouragement from my new companion, I stopped feeling inferior about my origin.

But Hosoda Obachan's condition wasn't getting any better. She couldn't continue her lessons, and without that income her savings were quickly running out. When her sister, Hiroshi's mother, visited us from the country and urged her to come live with her, Hosoda Obachan agreed. In late fall, Hiroshi came home from Tokyo to help us complete the move.

It was a difficult farewell for all of us. She didn't say much to those who came to bid her good-bye, but her eyes were wet as the train moved slowly away from us, and from the city that had claimed her talents and given a purpose to her life, which no amount of poverty or disease could erase.

To keep me from changing high schools again, my mother came to the city to live with me. My brother joined us, and we were a family again.

Now that I was released from my great responsibilities, my last year of high school was a happy one. Whenever we could, my friends and I would go to the beach or the mountains, attend a movie, or just walk around the city streets pretending to be tourists. Sometimes, like the girls I had seen my first day in the city, we acted like we owned the city ourselves. I belonged. I wasn't the country girl bungling her way in unfamiliar territory anymore. I was at home.

Many people who didn't live in Beppu City streamed into the city seeking pleasure, mementos, or something they could not name. Americans walked the streets with the dignity and right of way reserved for victors. Little children crowded noisily around them, shouting: "Give us something to eat.... Do you have any chewing gum?" Often, the soldiers rushed in and out of the city in their jeeps or sedans.

Men and women in all types of clothing—student uniforms, old-style kimonos, workmen, soldiers, and others in western dress—filled the city day after day, but rarely did I find on their faces the gentle, loving eyes I had known as a child in my village. Ambition and desire, hunger and thirst for something they did not have, were mirrored there instead. When I observed them, my great desire to know the reason for life increased.

After what seemed like half my life, but was only a little more than three years, my high school graduation day arrived. As the ceremony began, the principal and all our teachers stood before us one by one to give us their parting speeches. They spoke of our future, the condition of the world, and their hopes that we would be successful in curing some of the problems which the war and their generation had not solved.

Finally, according to prior announcement, a young American missionary stood up and began speaking in fluent Japanese. He used lively gestures and wore a continuous smile on his face. His tall appearance, dark blue suit, and pure white tie caught every eye in the auditorium. It was unusual to see an American in civilian clothes. Besides, he was an attractive, young man, and his loud, dramatic voice kept the audience at rapt attention.

I listened intently until he mentioned two very familiar words: heaven and hell. I was stunned. America and Japan were on opposite sides of everything else, but when I heard this missionary speak about sin and its consequences, and I remembered that my family had taught me the same things, we didn't seem like enemies anymore. We agreed on something—something terribly important, something that could help put the confused pieces of my life into logical order at last.

"If you steal a penny or cheat someone of even that amount," he said, "you are as guilty as if you had stolen a million dollars. Stealing is stealing no matter what the amount. If something is not yours and you take it, you are stealing, and stealing is sin."

I couldn't concentrate on his words anymore. I was remembering the time my friends and I stole a watermelon on the way home from school, and I suffered in my guilt. We had been so thirsty after walking six miles up and down the mountain, and there had been no one around to ask. The watermelon patch had attracted us all, and it was the most delicious fruit any of us had ever eaten—but it was stealing. I knew that at the time.

Not only the watermelon, but what about the time we found that money on the way to school? Instead of turning the money in to our teachers, we used it to have a party. And once I stole fruit out of my neighbor's trees to fill my empty stomach. Or how about when my mother and I made a gift box to hide some rice from the eyes of officials so we could carry it to our relatives in the city?

Oh, I had committed so many sins, and everyone else was doing similar things to recover in that lawless world after the war. I was certain now that not one of us would ever get to heaven. We were all destined for hell.

Again, like wanting to bring heaven down to earth for everyone to enjoy, my desire was to do something to turn everyone away from the road to hell. But now that task seemed impossible to me. I was in the world, too. I was doing wrong, too, and there was no hope for any of us. I had chosen an impossible dream.

While I was behaving like an active teenager, consumed by the excitement of my new life in the city, I had forgotten what my aim in life had been. Now this young missionary made me remember. He spoke about a completely different religion from the other side of the world, but it sounded so much like my own. I didn't understand all he said, but there was a sparkle to him that seemed to convey that there is hope, that something can be done to reverse the direction of a person's life, and even the direction of the whole world. I didn't grasp what that process might be, because my attention to what he was saying was interrupted by the intrusion of my own thoughts.

Suddenly my grandfather's life made sense to me. He had wanted to reverse the direction of the world, too. He wanted better education for his children in the midst of ignorance and superstition, yet he didn't confine his efforts to his own family. Perhaps he didn't intend to be a philanthropist at all, but because he knew he couldn't improve conditions for himself or his family without making life better for those who lived around him, he built the school auditorium and made other improvements to benefit all the children of the village. Nor was the road he carved from the town to the upper village for his wagons only, but for all who needed to travel in that direction.

My grandfather knew the secret. If you want to improve your own life, improve the lives of others. Yes, he knew, and now I knew. It was my moment in the relay race. My grandfather was dead, and the cup had been passed to me. Now I had to run with it while I still had energy and life so the chain would not be broken. I couldn't get sidetracked again or the race would be lost.

But now the questions returned. Where was I going in my section of the race? What procedure would I follow? Should I stay here in Beppu City now that my schooling was

finished, or should I return to the countryside? Should I....
Should I...? As questions continued to monopolize my
thoughts, another memory surfaced....

"What do you think of this story?"

My father and I had gone fishing that summer evening
to a nearby mountain stream. Frogs were croaking like a
mighty chorus, and he began to tell me a story, as he always
did when we were together:

Once there was a king frog who lived all alone in a
small, country pond. One day another frog came hopping
by and greeted him.

"How are you sir? asked the visiting frog. "What are
you doing in your pond on such a beautiful, summer day?"

The frog in the pond replied proudly, "I am very fine,
thank you. I am doing what I enjoy most—living in this
pond where I am the king. Everything here is mine. You are
welcome to join me."

"Thank you, sir," replied the visiting frog, "but I am on
a journey to find the king of the whole world. Why don't
you join me? We can learn about the world together."

"What a fool you are! Why should I bother to hop
around the world in this hot, summer weather when I have
everything I need in this cool pond where I am already
king?"

"I may be a fool, indeed," the visitor replied, "but someday I may meet the king of the whole world."

The conversation ended and the fool frog hopped away,
leaving the king frog, as he wished, alone in his own pond.

My father finished his story and turned to me: "Now,
which frog do you think was the wise one?" I was a second-
grader at the time.

"The king frog in the pond!" I said quickly.

"Was he?" My father wasn't satisfied. He looked at me with a quizzical expression, and I realized he had tricked me with the words "king" and "fool."

"I mean the fool frog!" As I changed my answer, I was laughing along with my father. I wanted to be right, to have him pleased with me, even though at the time I'm sure I had no idea how to tell a king frog from a fool. The trickery of the words had just made me laugh.

My father loved telling me stories. Always, I realized much later, there was a lesson to be learned from them. I had forgotten most, but now in light of the missionary's speech and my conclusions about my grandfather, this story's meaning came alive for me. I thought for a minute that the king frog was like my grandfather, who was a landlord in a small town. But, unlike the king frog, my grandfather didn't live there just to be by himself. He might not have gone to other towns or countries in search of kings or adventure, but he made it possible for those he educated or employed to enlarge their boundaries. By sending them away from their pond, so to speak, he was always on a journey himself,—a journey upward as he elevated the living conditions of those around him, and a journey outward as he thought little of himself while concentrating on the achievements of others.

I wondered about my father now, and what he intended to teach me from the frog story. Was my father seeking the King of the world? Is there a King of the world, and if so, where, who, what is He? These questions stirred other memories of my father....

Early one summer morning during the war, I awoke to an unusual stillness. No one else seemed to be in the house. I left my bed and walked outside, hoping to find someone there. It was barely sunrise, the air was cool, and the plants were still wet with a heavy dew. In the eerie light I saw my father silhouetted against a backdrop of the valley beyond our yard. He stood there with his head bowed toward the ground, and his hands clasped tightly in front of him. I decided he must be praying, and I made no effort to disturb him. I decided to pray, too.

Imitating my father, I put my hands together exactly as his were, closed my eyes like his, and stood beside him. When I sensed his movement, I opened my eyes and saw him looking at me, smiling with his gentle eyes, loving me, and waiting for me to speak.

"What are you doing here?" I asked hesitantly.

"I was praying to God," he answered.

"What is God?" I asked, curious about this invisible person or thing I had heard so much about.

"God is the Lord of all creation, the whole universe," my father said, a touch of wonder in his voice. I didn't understand.

"What are you praying about?" I wanted to know.

"I was thanking God for everything He has created, for the sun and moon, the stars in the night, the food we eat, for the rain that makes our crops grow—just, for everything."

But I still didn't understand. I couldn't see nor imagine this "God" who continued to invade my mind like a giant puzzle.

Now, as I sought the meaning of the frog story, I began to see some connection between the fool frog's search for the king of the world and that early morning conversation with my father. If there were a King of the whole world, He must also be what my father called the Lord of all creation. And if this God really did exist, then my father must have been on a journey to seek this King like the fool frog who had been trying to find the king of the world.

But my father was wise already. Why was he still searching for something named God? Was he wondering, too, how

31

to bring happiness into a world suffering from hunger and sickness in a time of war? Could my father, too, have been moved to seek this King because of his love for his family and the world? Had He been part of my grandfather's relay race, too?

Now, like my father and the fool frog, I wanted to find this King of the world, for if anyone could fix the world, it must be this wonderful person I couldn't quite define. I still didn't know how or where I would find this "God" or "Lord," and it still seemed foolish to me to seek something that was invisible and beyond my reach or ability to understand. But I kept thinking about those two frogs, searching for hidden meanings behind their significance and how those meanings applied to me.

At last I concluded that I ought to be like the fool frog, even if I were seeking answers to foolish questions and impossible dreams. I knew I wasn't wise anyway; there was too much I didn't understand. But I was suddenly very happy to continue the search my father and grandfather seemed to be on, and to let their desires come alive again through me.

So on the day an American missionary triggered long forgotten memories of my past, I graduated from high school with the solemn determination to step out of the pond-sized area of my life into the ocean-sized world beyond. I was satisfied to identify myself as the fool frog in my father's story. Like a cane in the hand of a person who is blind, my diploma and the guidance I had received from my father would lead me away from the small pond to a place where I could meet this God, the King of the whole world, someday. Or so I hoped.

I could hardly wait to begin.

Chapter 4
TOKYO

"Don't worry about the bicycle; I'll replace it. Let's go out this evening."

My boss was being kind, I thought. One of the bicycles, our only transportation for errands and deliveries at the small shop where I worked, had been stolen the day before. Since I was the only person on duty at the time, it had been my responsibility to keep the bicycles locked when we were not using them, but I had forgotten to do so. Now it was also my responsibility to replace the stolen bike. I didn't know how I would find the money.

I knew my boss had a wife and two sons, but, to be friendly, sometimes after work I would stop at a café with him for coffee. Occasionally we remained there for dinner. His wife was a kind person, too, though she suffered from some kind of sickness. I often babysat for her when she had to stay in bed and her maid couldn't come. So I thought his invitations were to thank me for my kindness to his family.

The shop was my second job in the year and a half since graduation. Before that I was a bookkeeper for a construction company, a task I had found very easy to do. But learning to live in the working world with so many types of people, I found, was not easy for me at all. I tried hard to meet each challenge, to improve myself, and to please my superiors, but I soon discovered not everyone shared my goals.

Laughter and kindness were common among my fellow workers, but so much of the time it was uncomfortable for me to be with them. Unlike the people I grew up with, their language seemed to lack sincerity. I called it "double-talk" because it had a sunny side and a dark side. Sometimes their words came across as flattery or gossip, and sometimes they were obvious lies. I felt I couldn't trust anyone, or even understand their thoughts. I compared myself to a plant raised in a hothouse and tended with care, but here in the outside world my shelter was gone, and I didn't know how to cope with my new life.

I missed my childhood, my leisurely walks, the days with Hosoda Obachan, and my school friends who had seemed so much like me. So when the opportunity came to change jobs and work in the little specialty shop as a book-keeper and cashier, I was certain the atmosphere would be more like my upbringing. But I was wrong.

Now in my weakest moment, when my conscience was troubled because I had made such a costly mistake and disap-pointed the man I worked for, he stepped in with his typical, sweet kindness—a kindness that now made me uncomfortable and confused. He didn't even mention the bicycle, but began talking about his unsatisfying marriage, which, he said, had been arranged by his parents. Not long into the conversation, he said he intended to divorce his wife someday and marry me. He didn't give me a chance to say what I thought of the idea, but asked that I think about it for the time being.

But such a thing was unthinkable to me, and, in those days, the worst kind of behavior imaginable. I felt sorry for his life's circumstances, but I wondered what would happen to his wife. Who would take care of her? The more I thought about helping my boss break up his marriage, the more my doubts about his sincerity increased. I even wondered if he had hidden the bicycle himself so I would feel obligated to listen to his sad story and say "yes" to his plan.

A few days later, without even asking for my pay, I told him I was leaving. Perhaps to get as far away from him and the disappointments connected with two jobs, I set my heart toward the big city, Tokyo.

Immediately my mother began to arrange my trip. Masayuki had already moved to Tokyo when the Red Cross transferred him to the Tokyo office, and I was happy that I would be living near him again. Still, I hoped I would find a job soon so I would be independent, and not become a bother to him and his wife.

My mother's eyes twinkled with tears as she stood on the platform with the others who had come to say farewell. Watching her, I thought of that earlier day when we had come to this city together. She wasn't going with me now. I remembered, too, when Hosoda Obachan had left the city, and I had come to this same platform to say farewell to her. Now it was I who was leaving, moving forward again into the unknown, and I felt very much alone.

It was late March, the season of change, just as it had been when I arrived in Beppu City. The station was unusually quiet, with fewer people waiting for the train and less commotion from the blaring horns and noisy street vendors of four years before. I recalled how afraid I had been then in my youthful sailor dress even with my mother beside me. This time, instead of my mother sending me on a journey, it was my idea to go, and I expected to feel much more confident about my decision. But as the moment of my departure drew nearer, I felt that familiar terror at the thought of starting life over again in the giant city of Tokyo.

I had obviously matured since then. Instead of my student uniform, I now wore the black wool suit which had been made from material I received for graduation. My black high heels were a gift from one of my brothers to match the suit. My shoulder bag had been donated by a neighbor, and I held my mother's suitcase in my hand. I had nothing of myself, just the swaddling reminders of those who cared for me.

To hide my feelings, I joked with those who had come to see me off. They teased me, too, saying I would forget all about them when I got to the "big city." My mother watched me constantly, her confident smile showing in spite of her glistening eyes.

The train chugged slowly into the platform, and it was time for me to go. As I climbed aboard I heard my mother's voice rising above the chorus of "*sayonaras*" and "take cares."

"I'll send the rest of your things soon....Give my love to Masayuki....Take good care of yourself."

I barely saw the empty seat by the window, or distinguished the sea of hands still waving to me as the train pulled away, because my eyes were flooded with tears. The faster the train moved, the more the tears increased. There was no use wiping them away; they fell continuously. Memories of my childhood and the past four years in Beppu City came and went as fast as the scenery outside my window sped by. Person after person, memory after memory, they were all so precious. Why couldn't that secure, happy part of my life go on forever?

"Young lady, why are you crying so much?"

The voice startled me, jolting me away from my reverie and back into the present. For the first time I noticed the middle-aged gentleman, sitting across from me, peering at me over his newspaper. His neatly combed hair was mixed with gray, and his dark suit communicated an air of distinction. A professor, perhaps? His eyes were soft and tender as he spoke.

I was deeply embarrassed and didn't know what to tell him, but I knew I had to stop crying.

"I'm going to Tokyo for a Congressman's meeting," he continued. "I usually take a third class seat when I'm traveling to save the government money. And where are you going?" he asked, folding his newspaper neatly and laying it on the seat beside him.

"Tokyo, too," I said, finally finding my voice.

"Do you know anyone in Tokyo?" he asked with concern.

"My...brother..."

"I see. Is this your first trip there?"

"Yes," I answered between unchecked sobs, knowing I must sound like a little child.

"Then that's why you are crying. You don't need to be embarrassed. Was that your mother—were they your friends who waved so long as you were leaving?"

"Yes, sir." I was almost my natural self again as the thought of all those exuberant people waving so erratically brought a smile to my face.

"Why are you going to Tokyo?" My seatmate was obviously curious about me.

"To find a job," I said with so much lack of confidence I was sure he would laugh. Instead he continued to probe gently with more questions.

"How old are you?" he wanted to know.

"Nineteen, sir."

"Oh, I have a daughter just your age. She is still in college. Well," he said, reaching for a small package inside his bag, "my wife made me some *Sushi* (sugar and vinegar rice, served cold). It's too early for supper, but would you like to have a bite to eat now?" He was so kind I began to choke inside again.

"No thank you, sir. I'm not hungry. My mother made something for me, too, but I can't eat," I managed to say, gesturing toward the *Furoshiki* (print cloth)-wrapped bundle beside me.

"If you are not hungry, then I will save my snack for later, too. We must be almost to Moji," he said, standing to stretch his back and legs.

I guessed he had been on the train for a long time already, and he still had a long journey ahead of him. Although the express train we were riding stopped only at the larger stations, it would still take us 24 hours from the city I had left to reach Tokyo.

With my eyes finally dried of their tears, I turned my attention to the scenery. I was fascinated as we skimmed the countryside between mountains at full speed. A few farmhouses passed my view, sparkling in the warm, early spring sunlight. Here and there herds of black cows grazed on a hillside, and added to the peaceful sight.

It wasn't long before I noticed small patches of green standing out in refreshing contrast to the dull, brown background, and I knew it was new barley, about three inches high. How vividly I remembered stamping down plants just like these with the farmer's wife when I was so young. She said it was good for the barley to stamp it down, so the plants would grow stronger and produce a finer quality grain.

Quietly I absorbed the lesson of the young barley plants as my own, sensing that I, too, was being stepped on and pressed down so I would be strong enough someday to be useful in this needy world. Hosoda Obachan must have been stamped down many times to become the mellow person she was, so full of kindness, always thankful and uncomplaining, and trying to please everyone she knew.

Before long the train entered another city and the scenery changed again. There were no cows, no signs of new life springing from awakening fields, only blue smoke rising from the acres of rooftops that dominated the landscape. Some of the passengers began to move around, preparing to get off. The friendly gentleman sharing my compartment was back in his seat.

"It's tiring to sit for a full day," he said, "but it's easier when you have someone to talk to."

I smiled at him through finally dried eyes. Somehow I trusted him.

"At this station so many people get on the train they usually fill all the empty seats," he said, "and the closer we get to Tokyo, the more crowded it will become. Perhaps you should put your suitcase on the overhead shelf."

I agreed, but before I could follow his suggestion, he took the suitcase and lifted it for me. Like a guardian angel, I thought. No matter how terrible any situation had ever been for me, I acknowledged, there was always someone in the midst of my troubles, a chosen one to help me or give me hope. I thanked the one who was helping me now, thinking briefly that I had my father with me again.

Just as the gentleman had said, this station was crowded with people, both those who were leaving the train and those who were getting on. Some were passengers, and some were merchants selling their boxed lunches, juice, tea, candy, or fruit, all advertising their products in loud, convincing voices.

This city was near where my other brother, Tatsuo, lived. He worked as a mechanic in a smaller city a few hours away. I knew my mother had sent a telegram to let Tatsuo know I would be coming through here today, but I wondered if he had received it in time.

As I scanned the platform looking for my brother's familiar face, I suddenly saw him peering into each window of the passenger car I was on. Soon he was almost at my side, and I began to gesture wildly. When he finally saw me he broke out in his remarkable smile, raising his hand at the same time to signal that he had spotted me. Then, with so many people crowding around him, he disappeared among them, and I couldn't see him anywhere. My heart began to pound and break again as the train started giving its first signal to move.

I felt a tap on my shoulder, and turned to find my kind travelling companion pointing to the train's entrance several yards from my seat. There was my brother inching toward me, struggling against the mass of people and packages clogging the aisle.

"Here, take this," he shouted, stretching painfully over the heads of half a dozen passengers and placing something in my hand, "and take good care of yourself. Give my regards to brother Masayuki and his wife!"

"How did you get here?" I called loudly.

"I drove the company car at full speed," he shouted back. With a final "take care of yourself" as the train began to move, Tatsuo turned and left the train as quickly as he had come.

I sank into my seat, aware that people were staring at me, my heart joyful and heavy at the same time. Unlike my older brother, Tatsuo often acted before he thought. I remembered many tales about him, all the way back to his childhood. What had just happened was so like him. He couldn't come to see me by catching a bus, so he drove the company car at full speed to get to me in time. But however he did it, he fulfilled his promise to our mother! I prayed for his safe, and slower, return to his city.

"That must have been your brother; his eyes were just like yours and your mother's." My traveling companion was caring for me again, smiling, sharing my happiness.

"Yes, sir," I answered proudly, as I started crying again. For the first time I looked at what Tatsuo had put in my hand. I was stunned to find a small, red purse with five thousand yen inside—more than a month's pay at my former job.

Five thousand yen! I had never had five thousand yen at one time in my whole life. What had he sacrificed to give that much money to me? Would he be able to get along without it? I could feel his love filling me to the bursting point. I still couldn't believe he had been there with me just a few moments before, but I had the red purse to prove it—and five thousand yen!

The familiar tears continued to flow, though more silently now and with a tinge of happiness, because I had been given such a devoted family. Perhaps someday I could give back as much as they were giving me now.

The gentleman opened his lunch and again urged me to eat, but I still wasn't hungry. I opened my small book to read, but it was useless. I couldn't concentrate, either. So I gave in to my emotions again, closed my eyes, and let the tears run down my face. I remembered my childhood with Tatsuo, how I followed him everywhere—up mountains, to the ocean or nearby streams, trapping rabbits or fish—everywhere he went. How pleasant were my memories of him....

The annual school athletic meet was in full swing. Tatsuo and the other fifth-grade boys were lined up on the starting line for the short distance race. I heard the signal and saw my brother running at top speed, taking an early lead. All the school children, their parents, and teachers were cheering from outside the racing ring.

Suddenly, at the half-way point, my brother fell. He had stumbled over something on the track, and the next boy stumbled over him. Other boys fell into the heap, too, but one by one they got up and continued the race. Finally Tatsuo got up, too, and in spite of the delay began to catch up with the others. Everyone cheered for him. He had lost too much time to regain his lead, but he managed to pass one runner and cross the finish line second to last. The applause for him was greater than it was for the winner.

Then in front of the startled, cheering fans, Tatsuo fell down again, slumping to the ground as though he were dead. For a moment there was dead silence. Then someone called for a stretcher, and a prearranged crew went speedily into action. I started to run toward him, but someone held me back. I glimpsed his face as he was being carried away on the stretcher and could tell he was alive, but I didn't know where they were taking him. He was obviously in pain. My grandmother had been able to reach him briefly, and I noticed her hands were covered with blood. Her face was dark with pain, just like Tatsuo's. I was terrified. Was my brother going to die?

No, I soon learned, he wasn't going to die. He had a four-inch cut across his knee from the sharp rocks on the racetrack. It took a long time to clean, stitch, and dress his wound, but by evening we knew he would completely recover.

In Buddhist teaching, my grandmother had taught us, you don't give in to defeat. If you fall, you get up again; if you fall seven times, you must get up and try for the eighth time. If you have a setback, you begin again.

My brother had learned his lesson well. It was so like him to fall, to experience trials or difficulties, but to get up again and go on until the race or the job were finished. He would not let pain, distance, or a train full of people keep him from reaching his goal.

Throughout the sleepless night and day of my journey to Tokyo, amid the clattering sounds of the train and the movements of the other passengers, I followed the chain of events of my life, and I cherished each proud moment. My train was speeding toward the largest city in Japan, into vast unknowns made even more frightening by the approaching dusk, and I needed to expand all I did know, all I had experienced, just to keep the terror from overwhelming me.

"We will be at the Tokyo station in another thirty minutes. Are you sure your brother will be there?" I caught the gentleman's concern.

"Yes, sir, I am sure because yesterday my mother sent

him a telegram," I answered, hoping myself that Masayuki would be waiting for me when I arrived. My brother was my only security.

The train with my thoughts and wonders arrived at the Tokyo station exactly on time. From the window my eyes raced across the crowd, trying to find my brother. The platform was the longest I had ever seen, and there were so many people no one would ever be able to count them all. I'll never find Masayuki, I thought. Maybe he hadn't come.

Just as I was about to panic, I saw him. Joy replaced my fear as he stood near my exit waiting for me to get off the train. He knew exactly which passenger car I was in!

"Your brother must be here," my kind companion said as he noticed the excited expression on my face and helped me with my suitcase. "That's good. Take care of yourself now. This is a big city, you know."

As I looked at him in thanks and tried to say good-bye, I noticed he was watching me with tenderness. My heart began to choke with such gratitude that I could only nod without any words and bow quickly before leaving him.

Masayuki was full of smiles as he stood there wearing my favorite checked sports coat, so I could spot him better, I thought. He hadn't changed at all since he lived with us in Beppu City. He took my suitcase and asked me about the trip.

"It was okay," I said, unable to say much as I kept thinking of the kind gentleman who had taken care of me. I caught sight of him only once after I'd found Masayuki, and he caught my glance, too. Then, as if satisfied I was in safe hands, he turned and disappeared into the crowd.

For a moment I wondered if my father had known that someday, somewhere, someone would be kind to his daughter in her time of need. I remembered how kind he had been to people, even to strangers, when I tagged along by his side as a small child. I noticed also that it wasn't always easy to accept kindness from a stranger, but his actions touched my heart. I wanted to be like him someday and pass his kindnesses on to someone else. I wondered if my traveling companion had a father like mine and wanted to be like him when he grew up, too.

Evening in this capital city was noisy and bright, covered, it seemed, under tons of neon-sign make-up. People were pairing off with those they had come to greet, some going home and some looking for temporary accommodations while they visited in the city.

I wasn't sure if I were coming home, or if I, too, were searching for some temporary place to stay. My childhood was behind me. My first work experiences were over. The kind gentleman had disappeared. My brother was married now. Perhaps it wouldn't be the same. I couldn't tell. Masayuki looked the same, but I wasn't totally comfortable with him.

Perhaps I was just tired from the trip. Why judge the entire future of my life by these few, tense moments. The city was brimming with opportunity. I might not know how to look for the King of the universe, or the Lord of creation, but at least the fool frog had made it this far on her journey.

My brother interrupted my reverie.

"Are you hungry?" he asked. "Sachie is preparing for our supper at home."

Chapter 5
THE GAMBLE

"If you can't even get on the train, why bother to look for a job? You'd never get to work on time!"

Masayuki and his wife, Sachie, exploded in frustration. Making room for me in their tiny apartment was bad enough, but going with me every time I went into the city to look for work had eroded their patience. I had to overcome my timidity, push my way onto the ever crowded trains, and find a job so I could move into a place of my own.

Hordes of people in post-war Japan poured into the train stations each day, hurrying as though compelled to match the speed of a city recovering from war. Crushing someone else just to get on a train was unthinkable to me at first, but eventually I rejected my well-mannered upbringing and started elbowing my way through the crowds like everyone else.

I found work as a clerk-typist at an American Army Base and moved into a one-room apartment attached to the back of an old food store. Although I had to share the kitchen with other occupants of the building, at last I was on my own. I was fortunate to find a place only fifteen minutes away from the railroad station, and conveniently located near stores where I could shop for my daily needs.

For awhile, settling into my new life made me happy. I formed new friendships and began building fresh memories. Occasionally my fellow workers and I would escape the rush of the city and go hiking in the mountains just as I did when I was growing up. The clear mountain air, the sounds of the birds, and the sight of clouds floating softly over our heads rested our minds as well as our bodies. We talked and sang as we walked or laid down beside a mountain stream. Compared to the mountains, any problems we had, at least momentarily, seemed very small.

Confusion, however, still held me in its grasp. The speed and direction of my life were so much like life in the city. Both the rebuilding of the city and my day-to-day activities were moving very fast, but in my search for answers about that life, the pace was entirely too slow. I could always find my way in the mountains, but back in the city, and on my inner journey, I felt I would never find my way.

To build something new, I noticed, something else always had to be destroyed. Tokyo had its new buildings, smooth highways, and modern shopping centers on the very sites that had been bombed and burned during the war. But the same thing was happening in people's hearts and minds. Greed and ambition flashed from the eyes of the formerly deprived, fortune-hunting people, as all kinds of human wisdom competed for personal gain and success in their own eyes. My country was fast resembling a jungle, where the stronger survived by stepping on the weaker. Cultural changes followed a similar pattern, trampling on the old to make way for the new.

Much of this effort to bring about a more wonderful society for Japan seemed pointless to me. The balance between reconstructing our homes and cities, while maintaining basic human relationships, was still missing in spite of intense efforts by so many to bring it about.

Four years after I arrived in Tokyo, the American military presence in Japan began to wane. As bases closed, jobs, including mine, were gradually abolished. Once again, like my country, I faced the depressing process of starting life all over again. "What now?" I wearily asked myself.

At the close of work one day when I knew my job was about to end, I sat down on a bench at the railroad station and watched the people as they passed by. Trains came, filled, and left, but it didn't matter. I was in no hurry. I sat for hours watching, wondering if those who hurried past me ever stopped long enough to ask questions about their lives, too.

Every face wore some kind of shadow—fatigue, sorrow, worry, or something I couldn't define. Their pain hadn't ceased with the end of the war. The peace that had been declared among nations didn't seem to have penetrated their hearts. Their eyes looked into empty space as they passed by. No one noticed me; I was part of the bench.

Women in fine clothing and proper make-up hurried by, and I wondered what was under the facade. Gentlemen in crisp business suits passed by, too, appearing confident, but not always conveying the happiness I expected success to include. Laborers with pale, tired faces seemed anxious to get home, or at least to exchange their accumulated dissatisfaction with whatever form of leisure took their minds off the jobs they performed, day after tedious day.

Everyone was on a journey—I was sure of that. How I wished I knew what treasure at the end of what rainbow beckoned the entire human race, so I could rush out to share it with them. What secret formula for happiness would erase the tired expressions, straighten the slumped shoulders, and peacefully resolve the conflicts which raged within us all?

My mind clicked into reverse and I began reflecting upon incidents, one by one, which had occurred since my arrival here....

As a country girl living in Tokyo, I was incredibly naive. I was fooled by anyone who held out his hand to me, those who looked blind or crippled, and especially the children.

47

No matter what the age or affliction, I could never refuse a request for help. Each need seemed real to me, and I often emptied my purse even when I had almost nothing left for myself. I always knew I was better off than they were. I went to pawn shops to sell books I had already read, or borrowed money from my friends until payday, because I barely made enough money for necessities, let alone enough to give away. Of course I was laughed at, but I laughed, too, thinking I was certainly the fool frog which my father had spoken about so long ago.

Once, when the money I had collected for an orphanage was stolen from my locked desk, I was particularly disturbed. I had been so careful. How could anyone rob children? Again I emptied my purse to replace the stolen funds. My stomach was empty for days.

Besides being fooled by those whose business it was to prey upon the sympathy of the naive, I was also cheated by salesmen who came to my apartment door with an assortment of products and tales of woe. I bought things I didn't need or couldn't use because I could never turn anyone down. I often wondered why I couldn't say no, like learning to push my way onto the train; but still my generosity continued, and I suffered the obvious consequences.

I felt like the farm woman's barley plants, but without the assurance that being stepped on was helping me mature in any way. Instead, I became bitter and increasingly angry with myself and the conditions around me as the days and weeks went by. I could see that I was the cause of my own unhappiness because of my inability to refuse any request for help, and my ignorance about the world and its people, but I couldn't seem to change. I had thought helping others would bring me happiness, but I wasn't happy at all. I finally admitted that, in my search for life's purpose—which I thought had been to improve the world for its people—I had failed. I wondered if there was any point at all in staying alive.

Alone in my apartment one night, I made a mental list of all the reasons why I should go to heaven, and a contrasting list of the baffling, unhappy things which I had encountered in my short life. The choice was obvious. Convinced that my decision was best for me, I took all the aspirin I had on hand and lay down across my bed, knowing I would wake up in that wonderful place where my grandmother was. How wonderful it would be to see her! This was the end of the road for the fool frog, I told myself as I prepared to die.

A train of memories moved slowly across my mind as I drifted into sleep. I wanted to let my family know that I did all I could, but that perhaps I just couldn't grow up, couldn't outgrow the dreaming, the fantasies of childhood. No one else seemed to struggle with their thoughts as much as I did. Now, I wouldn't have to struggle anymore....

Early evening of the next day I awoke—in the same apartment, with the same smell of food floating in from my neighbor's kitchen. I sat up and looked around my room. Everything was the same. I had even failed to end my life because I hadn't taken enough aspirin to do any more than give me an extended period of sleep. If I hadn't been so despondent I might have laughed at the irony of the situation. Because of my constant lack of money, I always bought only the smallest jars of medicine, including aspirin.

Nothing had been solved. All my problems were still with me. I still had no money, and I was still dejected and confused. But after my long rest I did feel refreshed, and something about my improved physical condition stirred a new determination in me to go on with my life—at least for now.

I stretched my arm across the bed and felt the wrinkled newspaper lying there. I picked it up and read: "Another loser commits suicide...with a family of four...." Although this kind of news was not unusual in those days, the word "loser" troubled me. Why was he called a loser? I read the story, amazed

49

at the similarity between this man and myself. We had both felt pressed down, at a dead end, without enough money, and with no apparent escape from our difficulties.

Abruptly I closed the newspaper, got up from my bed, and announced to the four walls and my own finally unstopped ears: "Enough of this! I will go on! I will care again—for myself, for the world, for other losers like me—for everyone who has any need at all."

Needing to stretch my legs after almost 16 hours in bed, I left the apartment and walked down the familiar street toward the railroad station and the business district. A "help wanted" sign in the window of a Chinese restaurant caught my eyes. Without hesitating I went inside and was hired immediately as a part-time dishwasher. At least I was assured of one meal a day which no one could cunningly take from me; it was part of my pay.

The world might call me a fool and a loser forever, but I no longer cared what anyone else thought. I had regained that unquenchable desire to continue my search for the meaning and purpose of my life.

The clock on the railroad tower read 10 P.M. when I finally stood up from the bench. Rush hour was past; only a few people remained on the platform.

As I stepped into the dark, October night, the faint, cold stars reminded me of Grandma Shigeta and the night she had brought the bag of rice to our home back in the village of my youth. I could almost hear her words: "There is no fear of the sunset for a night traveler—only the expectation of the sunrise."

But my journey was different. I was a night traveler no matter what time of day it was, and I didn't know my destination as Grandma Shigeta had known hers. My final memory on the bench, the suicide attempt, and new burst of

50

enthusiasm for life had occurred more than a year before. Now I had to admit again that, in spite of my close call, life was no better for me now than it had been then.

There were no answers, I decided. Those thousands of people who had passed by me tonight didn't appear to have answers, either. They were just busy getting somewhere— anywhere, driven by all their wants and needs. And besides those in Tokyo, or the generations alive today, there had been countless doctors, scientists, philosophers, and other great minds throughout the history of mankind, yet still the human condition wasn't getting any better.

At least, I was now certain, the answers to my questions couldn't be found among people. I couldn't blame them for not understanding the reason for my existence and the meaning of my life if I couldn't provide the answers for them, either. So, it suddenly occurred to me, I had to find my answer from a different source altogether.

Predictably, a few days after my meditation period on the bench, I was out of money again. Though I didn't want to ask my brother for money, I had no other place to turn, and I made the humiliating decision to ask him for a small loan until I was paid again. Even when I didn't give my money away or replace what was stolen, I could barely make it from payday to payday on what I earned. Living in the city was expensive.

Each month those who rode the commuter trains could purchase a pass allowing them to ride between certain points for that period of time. If we needed to ride beyond our particular destination, it was necessary to purchase another ticket for the extra distance.

My brother lived beyond the distance my pass allowed me to ride, but I didn't have money to pay for the extra ticket. I thought of all the money that had been stolen or cheated from me since I had come to the city, and my conscience dulled.

51

Many people told of flashing their pass quickly as they left the train, and the men in blue uniforms who inspected the limitations of the pass would be none the wiser. I knew it was wrong to cheat the railroad, but I felt I had no choice.

The train passed my usual stop, and soon I was at the station near my brother's house. My heart felt like ice as I stepped off the train. I imagined there were eyes everywhere who knew what I was doing, and they were all staring at me. My mother often spoke of "the eyes to see the truth" and I shivered at the prospect of being discovered. I wondered if there really were eyes somewhere to see the truth, and if there were, then besides seeing me perform this illegal act, they also had to know why I was doing it. They had to be able to see inside my heart and know how deeply I had been hurt by the world.

I struck a bargain with myself. If I were caught with the insufficient pass, I would continue my search for truth. But if I were not caught, then I would know there was no all-wise King, no "eyes to see the truth," no use to continue seeking Him or them, and I would give up my search. I would leave Tokyo and return home to the simple life of the countryside. I gambled my entire future on what I was about to do.

Holding my head high I walked through the checkpoint, displaying my pass in my upturned palm. Just one of hundreds pushing hurriedly through the passageway. How could my deception possibly be detected?

Perhaps it wouldn't be so bad after all to go home.

Chapter 6
THE PATH

As sudden and searing as a bolt of lightning, a stream of light flashed through me as I felt the grip of a man's hand on my wrist.

"Come with me," he commanded politely, pulling me carefully away from the crowd.

"Thank you! Thank you!" I stammered, remembering my grandmother had taught me to give thanks for everything.

The young man was startled by my strange response and looked at me questioningly. Recovering his composure, he pointed to a small open space nearby, and told me to wait there until he could route passengers toward another checkout point and close his. In spite of my terror, I liked the young man's professional manner. His dark blue uniform reminded me of my two cousins who worked for the railroad near my home town.

This time as I waited in a crowded railroad station, people were observing me. Some stared curiously, while others, embarrassed or relieved that it was I who had been caught and not they, avoided my gaze completely.

One chance in a million—one out of all these people. Nothing set me apart from them. I was Japanese; I wore ordinary clothing like theirs; I hurried as they did. My co-workers always bragged that they didn't get caught. Why did I?

Strangely, I wasn't embarrassed or even shaking anymore. In those few moments since the young man had let me know I wasn't going to slip through his observation net, a great sense of relief spread over me. If I hadn't been caught, then certainly there were no "eyes to see the truth," and, if there were no "eyes" nor any power behind the struggling, incomplete minds of the human race, then there was no hope for the world—nothing to keep searching for. I had gambled, but, as awkward as these thoughts were for me, I began to think I had not lost the gamble at all. Now, at least, I believed the answers that I had been looking for existed somewhere.

"Please follow me to the office," the young man said. He had finished closing his booth and was turning his full attention toward me.

The "office" was hardly more than a shabby cubbyhole. A middle-aged man, also wearing a dark blue uniform, sat behind a desk reading. He raised his eyes as we walked in, revealing a settled expression as though he knew what the younger man had to say before he uttered a word.

"This young lady—this is her pass...." Without further explanation, my captor placed my pass on the desk in front of the person I assumed was his superior and looked once more in my direction. Still nervous, I thanked him again.

"Is this your pass?" asked the man at the desk.

"Yes, sir, and I'm sorry. I didn't have any money. I'm on my way now to borrow money from my brother, and then I'll pay what I owe." My words sounded so clumsy.

He nodded to the young man, an apparent signal for him to leave. I watched until he closed the door softly behind him, feeling apprehensive now that I had lost his comforting presence.

Gesturing to an old wooden chair by the desk, the man invited me to sit down. Silently I complied, and waited for sentence to be pronounced upon me.

"It is the rule that you must pay a fine of three hundred and fifty yen. Do you know that?"

"Yes," I managed through humiliation and beginning tears.

"And I must keep your pass until you bring me the money. I also need your ID card if you have one." He spoke gently. I removed my ID card from my wallet and placed it on the desk with my pass.

"Is that all, sir?" I asked.

"Yes. You are free to go now, but come back as quickly as you can, so you won't be without your identification for very long." He looked tired. How many times a day did he impose such fines and deliver the same lecture to offenders like me?

"Thank you—thank you, sir," I stammered again as I stood up to go.

Barely fifteen minutes later I arrived at Masayuki's house, grateful that he was already home from work. He and Sachie welcomed me.

After hearing my need for money, and without question, my brother gave me the amount I needed. He hardly heard my promise to return it by the end of the month. My heart responded to his continued love for me. If I had become a burden to him, he didn't reveal it. Again I was overwhelmed to have been born into such a loving family.

When I returned to the railroad office, the middle-aged man was still there. As soon as he saw me he welcomed me with a broad smile. I smiled weakly in return, passed him the money, and stood silently, not knowing what to say.

"So you work at the American Army Base—is that right?" He was very friendly as he handed me my papers.

"Yes, sir, I do." He must have noticed the information on my ID card.

"Where are you from?" he inquired further.

"Beppu, sir," I answered cheerfully. His kindness made it easy for me to talk with him now.

"Beppu! I've been there," he responded excitedly. "It's a lovely place."

"Oh, yes, sir, I know. I often remember my high school

days there." I could sense he was trying to ease my stricken conscience.

I couldn't believe my foolish act had ended this way. Receiving forgiveness and understanding which I did not deserve, from a man I had not known until this afternoon, swelled my confidence in myself. I felt like I had grown an inch since I entered the railroad station the first time that afternoon.

"Well, take good care of yourself," he said. He must have seen my tears and decided to let me go. Kindness from others, especially strangers, weakens me, and the tears always come.

This incident became an unforgettable lesson to me. I resolved from then on to be understanding and forgiving to others when they, too, felt helpless and foolhardy as I did today because, I decided, all those who found it easy to forgive others must have learned their lessons in forgiveness in a similar way. My new understanding even made it easier to forgive myself.

As I walked back toward the train and my journey home, the gentle smile on the tired face of the man I had just left lingered with me. I wondered if he had been part of those mysterious "eyes to see the truth." How could I know? I remembered again how I had felt when the young man caught my wrist. Why had I stopped shaking when that happened? I thought of the flash of light that cut through my mind at the same moment. What was that light? It reminded me of a childhood dream....

Soon after my father's death I was sitting on the top step of our town's shrine, high on the side of a small mountain, thinking about the war and our enemy: What was the enemy like? Do they really have curly, yellow hair and blue eyes? When we pray to our God to help us win this war, do they pray to their God to help them win, too, and if they do, how can we both win? One side has to lose! In the process of reasoning, I remembered the God my father called, "the Lord of creation." I wondered where that God could be and why we have so many gods. These invisible gods made no sense at all to me.

How I missed my father! But I had to face the reality that he was no longer with me. I would have to find the answers to these questions myself.

Suddenly everything around me became very still. I looked at the shrine, at the landscaped grounds, the trees. Nothing moved. I couldn't even hear the birds—only silence.

I was gripped with intense fear and started to run like the wind down the long flight of steps. About halfway down I stumbled. Had I not miraculously caught my balance, I would have fallen the rest of the way and surely would not have survived. Reaching the bottom I kept on running, trembling all the way home.

That night I dreamed of falling in the darkness. Though I was in a standing position, I was falling on and on into a large, tunnel-like hole, so terrified I couldn't breathe. Just then a flash of lightning sliced through the sky over my head, contrasting starkly with the endless darkness below. Moments later I awoke, immensely relieved that the experience had been only a dream.

But I couldn't let go of that dream. Why had the sky been so near above my head after I had fallen so far in the darkness? I could still see the flashes of light in the graying sky indicating the sunrise would soon come. Trees swaying in the wind were wet and sparkling under the streaks of light, displaying a new freshness after the storm. Had I been pulled out of the darkness toward the lighted sky with a reverse gravity from above, or was I falling out of the light into the darkness because of the gravity beneath? I couldn't tell, but I was puzzled by that near-death experience long after I awoke from my dream.

Plodding home from the train station in the early darkness, still reflecting on the day's strange events, another memory from my childhood stirred its way into my thoughts....

Waking from my nap to the sounds of play, I walked outside to watch children climbing a persimmon tree near our neighbor's well. I wanted to climb, too, but there was no room left for me. I had to be content to sit by our Shoji screen and envy the others in their fun.

Before long rain started to fall, marring the sunny afternoon and sending all the children quickly into their homes.

When the short rain shower ended, I ran to the tree before the others could come back and take away my pleasure again. I climbed up to one of the big branches just as they did, and positioned myself to sit down and glory in my triumph.

But because of the rain the branches were wet, and my feet slipped out from under me. Seconds later I was frantically holding on to my former perch with both hands, dangling directly over a pile of rocks beside the spring where farmers washed their vegetables and clothes.

Except for an old man with a cane coming up the hill in my direction, no one was in sight. My small hands were no match for the slippery branch and I knew I couldn't hold on until the man could reach me. As I feared, the branch slipped from my grasp and I felt myself beginning to fall.

To my surprise I didn't land on the rocks or in the ditch at all, but in the arms of the old man. How could he have reached me so fast? He had been too far away. But there I was, safe in his arms. I can still remember how gently he put me down on the ground, as though I were breakable glass.

Were there always "eyes" somewhere, watching me, protecting me from danger—revealing truth? There were just too many incidents in my life which couldn't be explained any other way: the old man breaking my fall, the Congressman on the train to Tokyo, my family in dozens of situations, and now the official in the railroad station. Could all these events be coincidences, or were they directed by a power far greater than I could understand, and for the very purpose of helping me discover what controls the visible world?

By the time I reached my apartment I was exhausted—not from work, or walking, or even the experience with my pass. Like so many times before, I was tired from the questions which kept reappearing in my mind, and the futile feeling that I would never find their answers.

What is truth? I asked myself that question again as I lay on my bed to rest. My mind focused again on my mother's "eyes to see the truth." My eyes were open but the room was dark.

Gradually but unmistakably, two eyes like a shadow appeared out of nowhere, moved toward me, and seemed to settle behind my head and align themselves with my own eyes. I thought it was an illusion from my fatigue, or that my brain was overworked—or was this another of my preposterous dreams?

My mind was alert; I knew I was awake. In an effort to drive away what I couldn't explain, I forced myself to dwell on the things I did understand, like the happiness I had already known. I longed again for my childhood. The world was simple for me then: the streams, trees, birds, flowers. How good the wind had felt on my face as I watched the beautiful sky above me, and then there was that unforgettable soft fragrance of cherry blossoms at a family picnic. How I enjoyed playing with the flower petals and leaves, completely free from worry that someone might harm me, or I could harm someone else.

But I couldn't reverse time, and I couldn't make any sense of those eyes behind or inside my head! I still didn't know if someone were watching me from behind or controlling me from within. It did seem possible, though I couldn't be sure, that the "eyes to see the truth" really were at my back, watching me, guiding my steps toward my still unknown destination, where I would know the answers to my barrage of questions. But it might be only a trick of my mind because I was so tired. Perhaps I wasn't awake at all but dreaming. Oh, would I ever recognize the sunrise in my life if it dawned?

My strange dreams, and now this crazy illusion or whatever it was, led to thoughts about death. What does it mean to be dead, I wondered, something like I'm feeling now? I couldn't move toward the future with confidence or go backward to start my life again. I felt separated from the world, walking my journey alone with no footprints to follow. I was so alone and so lonely, so tired I could hardly take another step. Isn't that what it's like to be dead, to be unable to move anymore?

Well, a dead person couldn't think, so I must still be alive. Finally, as I had done so long ago with the word, "God," I concluded that there must be "eyes to see the truth" if there were the words "eyes to see the truth," and I chose to believe that those "eyes" were present with me in whatever form they chose to take. Although my belief wasn't strong, I expected those "eyes" to guide me toward truth and the meaning of life, no matter what I did myself. If I traveled in the wrong direction, the "eyes" would have to correct me. If I chose the correct path, then the "eyes" would take me to the place or the person from which I could learn the things I so desperately wanted to know. I had come this far, and now I had the will to believe and to continue my journey. I was at the point in my life where my mother had often said, "when you reach the bottom, there will always be a door open for you."

I knew it was ridiculous to depend on make-believe eyes, but was any other idea I had come up with any less so? For now, the words alone were sufficient for me to believe, but I still thought, what a conclusion! So typical of a fool frog like me.

Suddenly the whole scene with the eyes and my wandering thoughts seemed so funny to me that I laughed out loud. It was a long time before I could stop the giggles.

From beyond my own limitations, a ray of hope streamed into my dark hopelessness. Thus, again, in Japan's capital city of Tokyo, with the aid of "the eyes to see the truth," I had the will to continue my journey. The path of my life seemed to point forward even if, in the process, I should slide more deeply into the unknown.

As I drifted to sleep at last, I pictured the sun's rays breaking through the dark clouds after a summer storm, like a second sunrise of the day. It was all so attractively refreshing to my tired eyes.

Chapter 7
MARRIAGE

Faithfully, week after week, I traveled to the unemployment office to look for a new job. I was proud of my patience. Besides, I was confident the "eyes to see the truth" knew my needs and would lead me to just the position I could enjoy, as well as paying me for my efforts.

But, although I continued to hope, no job came my way. Perhaps I wasn't patient at all, but too fussy and stubborn to take whatever I was offered. When my finances began to dwindle, I surrendered my stubbornness and accepted a low-paying position as a typist with a camera export company.

Typist, did they say? For nearly a week, all I did was examine camera parts. When I complained, the office explained that I would only work with camera parts until orders began arriving from America. What I hadn't realized, as well as this position being a new job for me, the camera company was just beginning its business, too. So far, there was nothing for me to type. I felt betrayed, and angry with myself that because of my impatience I had taken the wrong job.

While I continued to work at my disappointing job, my girlfriend introduced me to a friend of hers, who was a soldier in the American Army. Tom (shortened name for Tsutomu) was a "*Nisei*" (second generation Japanese/American) from Hawaii. I learned that he had been raised in the country as I was, that he wanted to learn about Japanese customs and how the Japanese people lived, and that he was a very kind and gentle man. Because my girlfriend's pre-arranged marriage date was approaching, she couldn't continue to spend time with Tom. Her mother asked me to help him with his shopping and communicating with the Japanese people in her daughter's place. Since I was already acquainted with Tom, this request seemed natural for me to accept.

So Tom became a part of my life. Although we were deficient in each other's primary language, we understood each other from the start. We met often, going for walks or to the movies, in the company of our friends or just by ourselves. I liked his gentleness and the comfortable feeling I had when we were together. For awhile I forgot about my inner journey, and even my dissatisfaction with my job.

In early winter after meeting Tom, I caught the flu and couldn't get out of bed for days. No one knew about my high temperature and aching body because I couldn't get up to tell anyone. I had no phone, no medicine, and no idea how long I lay there until much later.

When I could move around again, I noticed an envelope under my door. I opened the letter quickly and discovered it was from Tom. He said he had come to see me twice, but my landlord told him I wasn't home. He further explained that he was looking for a Japanese bride and expressed a desire to marry me, and that he needed my answer right away because the Army was about to send him to another assignment. If I would marry him, however, he would request to have his tour of duty in Japan extended for another year. Also, he wrote, it would please his parents greatly if he could bring home a Japanese bride.

As I was reading the letter, for the first time in months, I became aware of the "eyes behind my eyes," watching each word, reading along with me. Perhaps it was this other "presence" that turned my thoughts now to areas of my life I had never considered before.

What is a woman? If I knew, and if I were to live a nor-
mal, woman's life, could I fulfill that role without becoming
a wife or mother? There was still so much of myself I didn't
know. No wonder I couldn't understand others or know what
human beings were really like.

I was attracted to Tom with a feeling I had never experienced before, but the love I felt toward him wasn't like the
kind displayed in books or movies. Instead, it was like my
feelings toward my family, only stronger. I had loved many
people since my childhood, and sometimes I was misunderstood by them, and misused because of my naivete. But
now, I desired a love that could understand my love, a love
that would walk with me farther than the six or eight blocks
near my apartment, or along the tree-shrouded lakes in
Tokyo's many parks. I wanted to build a life with someone,
to share goals and find answers to life's questions with
someone else instead of struggling on and on alone.

And what is marriage? I also asked. I thought of my aunt
and uncle whom I had visited often during my summer vaca-
tions, and who seemed to support each other with a deep,
quiet love. I was like their own child as I shared their home
and played with my cousins. Yes, I wanted to build that kind
of home if I married. But how could I know if this man were
the one with whom I could achieve that kind of home?

In spite of my questions, it seemed logical to marry Tom.
Even my personal search for answers to my tumult of questions seemed less important in comparison. Still, I didn't
want to make a mistake. I was at least wise enough to know
that waiting for the right marriage partner was more important than choosing the right job. A mistake there couldn't be
corrected by giving two weeks' notice!

Was I being guided again? Were the "eyes" still there,
telling me to take a journey beyond my country in order to
learn about all the things I wondered? If so, then this marriage

was more than I could have asked for. If I could have a husband to share my life, and a family of my own to love along the way, how joyous a journey it would be no matter what I faced in the process.

I thought of my father's frog story again. Now, details which didn't have much significance before, took on new meaning. Each frog, I decided, had tried to persuade the other to do what he was doing. The frog in the pond invited the frog on the journey to stay in the pond with him, while the frog on the journey asked the frog in the pond to come with him on his journey. Why was this? Because, I concluded, each was lonely by himself. I could also identify with the frogs in another way. Whether traveling to a known or unsure destination, or remaining in familiar surroundings, life is terribly lonely when there is no one with whom to share the simple journey of life.

I had to believe now that the man who wanted to marry me didn't come into my life at this time without a reason. My heart was not in my job. Could it be that the "eyes" had not meant for me to look for a job in the first place, that all along, this force I still didn't quite understand, had other ways to meet my needs—marriage perhaps?

Everything seemed to conclude that I marry Tom, with one exception—my mother. I knew she would not be in favor of the marriage and would probably try to stop it. How could I blame her? I was her only daughter, and the man I wanted to marry would take me away from her for years at a time—perhaps forever. I didn't want to break her heart, or enter into marriage without her approval, yet Tom needed my answer soon because of the decisions he needed to make in his life.

Like so many times before, I laid my tired body on my bed, and wrestled with still another set of seemingly unanswerable questions.

Memories, precious memories of my mother poured

through my mind: the days we picked mushrooms, mountain vegetables, or flowers together; the times we went to the ocean for clams or seaweed; and the day she took me out of school so we could go to a nearby city to see the movie, "Bambi"....How I loved her! How could I break her heart when she had done so much for me? Still, it occurred to me, without Tom, my heart would be broken, too. Since her love for me was as strong as mine for her, I knew she would be just as sad about making me unhappy as I was about hurting her.

Two memories stood out from the rest....

My math homework that day consisted of ten problems. The first one was very difficult, but the other nine, I could see at a glance, were very easy. Out of habit, I started with problem number one, and worked on it for hours. Long after midnight I finally solved the problem, but by then I was so exhausted I went to bed without completing the other nine. When grades were announced at the end of class the next day, I had ten points while the rest of the class nearly all had ninety.

My mother was astonished. "If you could do the first problem, why couldn't you solve the other nine?"

"I knew I could do the other nine, so I started with the hardest one. Then," I continued to explain, "it was so late I couldn't stay awake to do the rest."

She was not impressed with my logic. "You should have worked the easy ones first. Then you would have had at least ninety points and, possibly, you would have stayed up until you finished the difficult one. Then you would have received a higher grade." This wasn't the first time she had been frustrated by my way of doing things.

"But, Mother," I argued, "anyone can see that if I could do the difficult problem I could certainly do the others. Besides, no one else in the whole class could do the first one," I said proudly, if not rebelliously.

"Life isn't that simple," she continued. "If you decide not to do something just because you know you can, then many things will be left undone in your life. Is that wise?"

I was silenced, even though I didn't fully understand what my mother was trying to say in those youthful days of my life.

The other memory concerned the day my mother received a letter which caused her face to light up like a happy child.

"She's coming! She's coming to visit me!"

"Who, Mother? Who's coming?" I was as excited as she was.

"My favorite teacher," she exclaimed.

Then my mother began telling me about this unusual woman. She told me about the time this teacher was studying hard to obtain a higher degree in her profession, but she became the laughing stock of all the other teachers. She was attempting to write her final report on a subject no one had ever written about before, and she was having difficulty gathering information. There wasn't much time left, and it didn't seem possible for her to accomplish her foolhardy goal on time. No one believed she would do it. She was the center of campus gossip.

To everyone's surprise, this teacher completed her report on her chosen topic, on time, and with surprisingly high scores. There were profuse comments about her work. When my mother asked how she had gathered her information, the teacher explained that she had simply disguised herself as a housemaid, gone around the city where she lived, and gathered the information firsthand.

"She became very famous among us, and was respected by the very people who had originally laughed at her. Isn't that ironic?" my mother asked me. "But she had an iron will about her, and a purpose she believed in. And if you aim toward something," she said, turning her attention entirely to me, "you must give everything you have to that goal. If you do, there is no way anyone can stop you from reaching it."

I was anxious to meet this woman and find out what kind of person would be so determined to achieve so much. But when I saw her, I was shocked. Instead of the strong, proud person I expected, I observed an old lady, wearing a simple kimono, with a soft smile on her wrinkled face. Her manner was so meek that I couldn't believe she was the same person my mother had spoken about, or who had had such courage in her younger days.

As I faced the decision about my marriage, I realized I was caught between those two lessons of my mother's. Marriage was the ordinary way of life for a woman, caring for a home and family, something most women eventually do. On the other hand, my inner journey—that search for answers—seemed indescribably difficult for me. However, if I followed my mother's teachings, I had to do both. I could not turn around and go home because I didn't finish my search, nor should I turn away from the ordinary thing just because it was something anyone can do.

This was my time to have that iron-clad will, to follow after ambition even though my mother might oppose me. After all, I convinced myself, these were her teachings, and not my ideas at all.

So I made the decision to marry Tom, knowing that I would manage somehow to accomplish both aims of my life, the difficult one and the ordinary one. I wouldn't forsake one to accomplish the other; I would achieve them both.

When I was strong enough, I went to the telephone booth near my apartment and gave Tom my answer. Soon we were making marriage plans. His eyes shone with delight as we talked. Despite the problems, I had never been so sure of anything as I was that I wanted to become his wife.

"Why do you have to get permission from your mother or brother to marry when you are already over twenty-one?" he wanted to know.

I wasn't very successful in explaining the reason to him, for I didn't really know what it was myself. Later, I realized, I was following a strongly entrenched family and national custom, one which I could not easily ignore.

"I will marry you anyway," I said, "but first we must try to get their permission. They might agree with me, or they might not, but I'll feel better if I let them know I want to marry with their blessing."

After a long discussion, Tom and I decided to talk with my brother first, and ask his help in approaching my mother. We took the train to my brother's house the next day.

"It won't be easy," Masayuki began. "If you are asking for her permission, you will never get it. You remember how difficult it was with my marriage, and that was only because Sachie's and my backgrounds were different. Besides marrying a foreigner, you are the youngest child, and the only daughter. I know she will try to stop this marriage."

My brother spoke bluntly, but accurately, as he described the difficulties we would face. He knew from his own experience that she would object to my marrying according to American culture, without a traditional matchmaker who brings two suitable prospects together.

"Then, what do you recommend I do?" I asked. "Can't you show her how well your marriage has worked? Tell her that times are different now; convince her how happy I am to have met Tom."

My mother's blessing meant so much to me that I found myself begging my brother to help me plead my case with her.

"Well, I can write her a letter, but you must tell her you

want to marry Tom yourself. If she doesn't agree to the marriage, there is nothing else you can do. If you want to marry him, then you will have to do it without her approval."

It was obvious that, after working with Americans for so long, my brother had adopted American thinking in many ways. I was startled by his sharp words, but I knew he was right. I had to tell my mother myself that I wanted to marry Tom. The air of certainty in my brother's voice convinced me that I had to stand on my own two feet at last. I could no longer depend on him or anyone else for the decisions of my life.

Though fully expecting my mother's disapproval, I wrote her my intentions. I also explained Tom's problem with the Army and why we needed her answer right away.

She didn't respond to my letter at all, but wrote to my brother of her strong disagreement with what I wanted to do. Masayuki handed her letter to me. When I had finished reading, he looked lovingly into my eyes and said, "I like Tom. And just think, you'll be seeing that lovely island of Hawaii any day now!"

I tried to smile. I knew Masayuki was trying to lift my heavy spirit, but I kept feeling the cold wind blowing mercilessly through my heart, not from the outside like that wintry day in my childhood, but from deep inside of me.

Tom sensed the pain I felt at putting my family aside to marry him, and he comforted me. I realized his love was slowly overtaking theirs as we spent more and more time together, planning our future.

Finally we proceeded with our paperwork to get married. In the process I discovered I needed some important papers from my mother, and I wrote to her again. Days went by and still she didn't send the papers or respond. Time was getting short since Tom's tour of duty in Japan was limited, and I was most anxious for her reply.

All of a sudden my mother arrived in Tokyo. When Masayuki left a message for me through the landlord that she was there, I became weak all over. According to my landlord, my brother demanded that I come to his house as soon as possible. Tom was braver than I, and he gladly went with me to meet her.

Though I expected the worst, to my amazement the circumstances changed completely when she met Tom face to face. They liked each other from the first moment as they spoke and laughed together, using my brother as an interpreter. She also brought the necessary documents, including a copy of our family census which I had requested.

Finally she turned to me and with a tender voice said, "He is a very nice man. You will be happy with him. He reminds me of the boys in the countryside where we lived." Her mood changed as she continued:

"It is sad that we cannot have a big wedding for my only daughter's marriage. I can't even give you anything for a wedding gift. But we can have a little family wedding for you right here at your brother's house before I go home. I must know what to tell our relatives. If you marry before I go home, it is easier for me to tell them. If you are not yet married, I would have to tell them the date of your wedding, and you know that will be difficult for you. Word will spread that you are going to marry an American and some will try to stop you. Others will talk about the kind of wedding you will have, and how sad that it won't be typically Japanese. You know how their minds are...."

As I listened to her, I began to understand her difficulty, as well as the great cultural differences between East and West. It would have been impossible to have a wedding that would satisfy all our relatives, who had so many different lifestyles themselves. It also would be hard for my mother to have a wedding when she couldn't afford it financially.

My mother put herself in my place in order to permit me to marry Tom, and now she was asking me to put myself in her place to spare her unnecessary heartache and worry. She was acting on what she had taught me, not to judge another person by one's own limited experience, but to put ourselves in the other person's circumstances to help us understand that different point of view. Perhaps, for her, the most painful part of my marriage was not my marrying an American, but feeling she had nothing to give, including a traditional wedding for her daughter.

But I was overwhelmed by the best gift of all, her acceptance of my decision to marry Tom. I wanted nothing else. This was more important to me than a traditional wedding. I knew my mother hadn't been able to benefit from any of my father's pension funds because of the loss of witnesses and the necessary documents during our postwar confusion, which would have confirmed his work as a teacher in a public school. It was a miracle to me that any of us, my mother and her three children, came through that difficult time with all its crime, disease, and shortage of food. But we did survive, even without any income, for almost ten years. I watched my mother sell her possessions, one by one. With that memory, and at this point in my life, the lives of those I loved were more important than material things, or the traditional wedding ceremony—which I didn't understand anyway.

Tom and I gladly agreed to marry while my mother was in Tokyo. It was far more than we had dared to hope. My mother's blessing and her wisdom were the crowning factors to both of us that our marriage was the right thing to do.

So we were married—simply, but with peaceful hearts—and entered a door that opened into a new dimension in both our lives. Tom's family couldn't come to Japan while we lived there, but we became acquainted through pictures and correspondence. We were happy that both our families had accepted our marriage. Once again my heart was filled with the warmth I had known all my life from my own family. I had lost nothing, and gained so much.

In spite of many technical difficulties—months of paperwork to satisfy American laws so I could become a legal, military dependent—our marriage began. In one sense it was a marriage of confusion, a union begun where two cultures met, and rules had to be broken or simplified under a canopy of love. But it was also the beginning of my journey into womanhood, a kind of side trip while walking the other journey to discover the purpose of my life as a human being.

"Be a good wife and make him happy....He is a nice, honest man."

My mother's words rang in my ears and I was comforted by them. Tom was happy to be with my brothers who, with my mother, made every effort to visit us since they knew we would soon be leaving Japan. I was still the spoiled, youngest child in the family, so I continued to be given more than my share of love and attention.

In mid-summer of the following year, our daughter, Gail, was born. My mother, brothers, and their spouses expressed their joy over the event. They almost forgot about me, and turned all their attention to her. My mother was with us for three months, helping me adjust to the experience of being a mother myself. During that time I was tempted to tell her of my inner journey, but I couldn't find the words to begin. I thought my explanation would be too abstract, and I was afraid to mention something I could hardly explain to myself. But I felt that one day I would reach my unreachable destination, and that, by achieving that goal, I would somehow repay my family for the love which they had sacrificed for me. I was determined again to go forward with the remainder of my search just as intently as I had traveled this far. Like my impossible marriage and the blessing of my family, I knew someday I would reach my goal, though I still sensed it would not be easy.

While watching my mother care for our baby, I experienced indescribable anguish. Someday I hoped I could explain everything to her, but for now, I knew I would have to say nothing. I sensed the "eyes to see the truth" knew every feeling being expressed in my heart.

I was happy in my husband's gentle love, and his nearness. Even in our disagreements we learned more about each other, coping with every new situation we encountered. It was indeed a happy life, this adventure of being a woman.

Time moved quickly toward the time of our departure from Japan. As we prepared to leave, I began to feel a new excitement for my new experience in the land called, "America," the land of freedom, the country of "in God we trust," as I had learned in high school.

It was mid-summer of 1960 when we finally stepped into the Pan American jet at Tachikawa Air Base near Tokyo, and I left my country and loved ones behind—cutting off one set of feelings in order to chart a completely different course toward another set of unknowns.

Gail was a year old as she lay in my husband's arms. I was twenty-six. The midday sky was cobalt blue under the blazing summer sun.

CHAPTER 8
AMERICA

I felt like a carrier pigeon on its maiden mission as our plane roared away from the Air Base, circled the city of Tokyo, and pointed its nose toward the sky. The ground beneath us rapidly resembled a miniature garden in a typical Japanese home. Soon, Japan itself looked like the small pond in my father's frog story as we climbed higher and higher, and moved farther and farther away from my homeland.

Before long the soft, cotton-blanket clouds blocked our view completely, and I could see nothing on the earth at all. The sun sparkled like a thousand prisms, and the sky turned a deeper blue than I had ever seen before. I could hardly believe I was actually in that space which had caught my attention so often from the ground.

The first flight of my life was a mixture of sadness and hope. Certainly the thought of my new home with my husband and child in that great land of America was joyful, but how I would miss my people and my country!

By now, however, I had learned that if I wanted to keep on learning new things, I couldn't remain in one place for very long. So I knew it was time to move on to yet another unknown destination in order to search for more parts of the mystery I was unraveling. I had been lonely before, afraid and unsure of which path to take before. I had suffered before, too, so I knew I could endure new situations, however strange they might be. And I didn't feel I was leaving my country forever. Someday, I planned, I would return to my motherland to share the discoveries I had made in America.

But what if I didn't return? That possibility tugged at my conscience and triggered a different kind of sorrow. In contrast to the white clouds outside my window, this new thought hovered like a dark cloud inside my heart. For a moment my sadness was overshadowed by guilt because I still had nothing to give my loved ones in return for their years of caring for me. If I didn't find the answers to my questions, or if something were to happen to me before I could return, this could be my first and last farewell to the family and country I loved as part of myself.

Though I knew my decision to marry Tom had included the possibility of moving far from all I had known and loved before, and though it made no sense to dwell on something it was too late to change, my brooding turned into an overwhelming sadness which gripped me and wouldn't let me go.

"When our loved ones die, they are not gone from us forever, but they return in their spirits to comfort us." My grandmother's words, still alive and embedded in my memory, suddenly returned to me. Soon came more words and memories of those who had already died, or those still living whom I had just left behind, and I realized the truth of what I had been taught. Whether living or dead, all my relatives were present with me now in my thoughts and through the guidance they had given me throughout their lives and mine.

And, adding a little wisdom of my own, if my loved ones were still with me, then I must still be with them, too. If we were bound together in our spirits through our love, then I didn't need to feel either sadness or guilt. So, confident that my family desired nothing but the happiest life possible for me, and I wished the same for them, the weight which had burdened me almost since we left the ground fell from my shoulders. Now the cloud in my heart was as white and blanket soft as the ones outside which, symbolic of both my family in Japan and those seated beside me, seemed to be holding the plane and all its occupants in their arms.

"If you love your child, send him on a journey...." The familiar words made sense to me now. This was how I was to know the value of my family and the depth of their love for me. I understood now that whoever believed this Japanese proverb and acted upon it must have complete confidence in their love for their child. It was that love that would be tested now, and the method by which their teaching would take root in the heart of that child who loved them so much.

As I emerged from my somber, emotional pit, my attention turned again to the plane soaring above the clouds, thundering toward my new homeland. Just like me, I smiled. I was free to soar, too, and to continue my journey toward the approaching sunrise of my life.

My daughter jumped cheerfully on my lap, and laughed as nearby passengers toyed with her. There was no sadness in her heart, and her joy spilled over to Tom and me. With the courage and trust of my new family, I was suddenly very content to build our own home in that unseen land of America.

Exhausted by the events leading up to our departure, and by the emotional gymnastics which seemed about to subside, I leaned my head on my husband's shoulder to rest. Seeing me close my eyes, Gail knew it was time for her nap, too. The plane's engines droned on, lulling each of us to sleep as we continued our journey together.

After a month in Hawaii with Tom's family, we boarded another plane for the Continental U.S. and our new home. How difficult it was to say "aloha" to that lovely Pacific island, and to the people who enlarged my heart even more with their love. In addition to the beauty of the island with its special fragrance and paradise of color, perhaps the fact that Hawaii was in my familiar Pacific Ocean had something to do with my reluctance to leave. These thoughts lingered with me as we took to the sky again.

Our first stop in the land of America was the city of Oakland, California. After the tedious process of locating our luggage and going through customs, and tending to Gail's needs, I realized I was actually breathing American air. We still had miles and days to go, however, before our journey ended. About all I could think of was how thankful I was not to be traveling alone. I'd have been lost for sure.

First, I remember, we were rushed by taxi to a smaller airport where we caught a military commuter plane to a rail-road station. After two nights and a day on the train, we reached Washington, D.C., where we summoned yet another taxi to take us to the Greyhound bus station. Two hours and a bumpy bus ride later, we arrived at our final destination of La Plata, Maryland. I was so excited I hardly noticed my exhaustion.

I observed my new land of America from all directions, amazed by its size and diversity, still disbelieving that I was really seeing it with my own eyes. For years in Japan I had heard about this great land, and now I was here. Was I dreaming? Were we really living near her great capital city, seeing her mountains and oceans, and meeting her people? The view from every highway stretched for miles. The homes and buildings were so different from those in Japan. Signs were written in English, farmlands were gigantic, and the public restroom door wouldn't open for me unless I put a dime in it. Even after I put in my dime there were no paper towels to dry my hands, and I wondered why this wonderful country would take my money but wouldn't give me a towel.

My quandary turned to laughter when someone explained what an "air dryer" was. Now I had another reason to identify with the fool frog. I certainly came from a small pond, I acknowledged.

People were so kind, helping us find a temporary place to live, and loaning us dishes, towels, and an old wringer washing machine until our goods arrived from Japan. Everyone was so friendly, too, banishing my fear that Americans would think of me as their enemy. I sensed their interest in us was genuine, even as they stared at us when we strolled through a shopping center or met them in a public place.

"What a cute daughter you have. How old is she?" a woman asked as we waited one day for Tom to attend to some business.

"Almost fourteen months," I answered shyly, conscious of my broken English.

"What a pretty girl you are," she said to Gail. "Here, I have something for you." She placed a small, round object in my daughter's hand and hugged her softly.

Gail's eyes were puzzled as she took her gift, studied it briefly, and then showed it to me.

"Thank the lady, Gail," I managed to say. Gail obeyed with a curt, Japanese sounding "Than-chu."

By the time Tom returned, the woman had gone, but I excitedly told him every detail about the encounter. I asked him what the gift was that she had given our little girl.

"Why, it's a silver dollar!" he exclaimed. Tom was as moved and grateful as I that his family had been accepted in his country.

"Be kind to others, even to strangers," my grandmother had taught me. This strange woman's kindness was repeated over and over as we settled into our new community. Sometimes the gift was a lollipop, some pennies, or a kiss on my daughter's cheek. I thought it strange that these

Americans were doing what I ought to be doing, that I was receiving instead of giving as I had been taught to do. I wondered, how did these Americans know about the teachings of Buddha and the customs of my people?

Perhaps my grandmother knew that one day I would be among strangers. But whether she knew it or not, she had prepared me for this journey into this strange land. Now, because those I thought would be different from me in every way were acting so much like my own people, I began to feel at home in the little town of La Plata, in the great, free land of America.

After several weeks in our temporary home, we found an apartment in the country, not too far from town or the Army Base where Tom worked. We were happy as we moved into our very own, two-bedroom apartment over our landlady's garage.

Mrs. Moore was an influential widow who owned extensive property. From her backyard we could see the Potomac River at the bottom of the hill. Her white house with its black roof stood tall against the massive oaks surrounding it on all sides. More than two hundred years of history were authenticated by that house.

Mrs. Moore was a heavy set, cheerful, well-mannered woman in her late fifties. Soon after we were settled, she took us on a tour of her expansive yard, while her handsome collie dog followed behind. Gail was delighted with the dog, her new playmate that was bigger than she was.

"Just make yourselves at home, and enjoy the whole place while you live here," she said. "I'm glad to have you here. If you need anything, just let me know."

Included in her introduction to our new home was the welcome news to Tom that he could fish and hunt on her property, too. And I was happy to know I could raise my very own vegetables and flowers close to our apartment. We couldn't possibly have found a spot more lovely, or more suitable to our needs. Even Gail had the collie dog, and such a large space in which to enjoy being a child.

"Never waste the kindness of others. Receive it with thankfulness; make good use of it...."

Again, the teachings of my family were translated into useful advice for my new life. I intended to make good use of all our landlady's kindness, for I loved this peaceful countryside away from the bustling activity in town. The air was clean with a sweet smell of the forest. Birds flew and sang everywhere, and the cows lying down just beyond our fence completed my picture of serenity.

As we finished our tour of the property and were about to part from Mrs. Moore at the front of our apartment, an elderly black man appeared from behind the house.

"Oh, Hazell," she called. "Come and meet our new friends. They're going to be with us for awhile in the garage apartment."

Hazell was a small man, well-tanned and healthy looking in his work clothes. Mrs. Moore introduced him as her gardener. He shook our hands warmly, acknowledged the introductions, and returned to work.

"No one knows exactly how old Hazell is," Mrs. Moore said. "He doesn't even know himself, but he is over ninety."

As she added information about her gardener, her large, blue eyes tenderly followed the small, black figure until he disappeared again around the house. The kind lady and her obviously faithful gardener completed the lovely picture of a Maryland countryside which has remained in my mind always.

Hazell became my good friend and advisor as I attempted gardening in American soil for the first time. He also became Tom's hunting guide—and our entertainer, as he recounted adventure stories from his long life. He loved our daughter, too, and frequently brought her pennies when

81

he came to my kitchen for a cup of coffee. We discovered, too, that he was a talented harmonica player, as he serenaded us on the porch steps of the main house during the twilight of our summer evenings. When Tom bought a second-hand washing machine, I offered to wash Hazell's clothes to show my appreciation for his kindness to our family. His eyes twinkled as he accepted my offer, just like the old folks of my childhood.

Mrs. Moore became our wonderful friend, too. Her caring heart showed in many ways—introducing me to her other tenants, and to her friends at a garden club meeting, and bringing us a delicious fruitcake for Christmas. I had little time to feel sad or lonely, for everyone made us feel at home and a part of their family. Soon I lost my identity as an outsider.

As the seasons changed, the well-kept grounds around my new home changed, too. Many different flowers bloomed to replace others whose season had passed. Throughout that first year I saw forsythia, iris, roses, lilacs, pussy willows, peonies, apple blossoms, and many more. I added petunias, pansies, and morning glories myself.

Eighteen months after we arrived in this idyllic, Maryland town, it was time to say farewell to these wonderful people and this lovely place. The Army had ordered my husband to go to Vietnam, and I would wait for him at his parents' home in Hawaii. But, the little town of La Plata, Maryland, had opened my heart to the American people, and etched a deep impression as I began my new life among them.

Ten years later, when we passed through this small town again to show our first American home to our daughter and, by then, our son Steven, the Moore place was unusually quiet. The gentle collie dog didn't come to meet us, and there was no sign of Hazell. When we walked around to that familiar backyard where I spent so much time with my daughter, we found a round swimming pool at the far end of the lawn. A tiny, yellow duckling swimming alone in the pool was the only creature there to greet us.

The duckling comforted me somewhat, but sadness was the stronger emotion. This wasn't our home anymore. Just like my childhood which I could never recreate, the days in our lovely Maryland countryside were gone forever, too. But the memories gathered there joined those of the other joyful periods of my life, and they were locked in my heart forever.

"Be thankful for all things...." The teaching of my grandmother echoed in my mind, and I had no difficulty obeying them.

Thank you, La Plata!

Chapter 9
THE TOUCH

Moving again so soon after my arrival in America was only a taste of what military life for our family would become. But, I thought, my inner journey would go on no matter where the United States Army decided we should go. My questions and I would always be at the same address.

Hawaii and a year with Tom's family helped soften the blow of our separation while he was in Vietnam. There the mountains are always green, and the comfortable wind from the ocean adds rhythm and life to the colorful flowers and tropical vegetation beneath a constant, cheerful sun.

But neither the loveliness of the island nor the kindness of her people could make me as happy as the first time we had come there. It was difficult to absorb the beauty around me while I was constantly worried about my husband in a war zone (my memories of another war were still too vivid), consumed with the care of a three-year-old, and awaiting the birth of our second child. In the midst of what should have been paradise, when I stood under the coconut trees, watched the peaceful, monotonous waves, or sat on the front porch of our rented house near my in-laws, my mind was often heavy and dark.

As the seasons changed, bananas ripened, mangoes and

avocados grew in size, and papayas and pineapples smelled wonderful in the distance. Tom's family and friends visited me constantly, always bringing samples of their fruit and flowers with them. How could I be unhappy? I was lonely for my husband, though I knew I had married a soldier and, thus, had accepted this separation as a part of my new life. But the news which entered our living room each day from Vietnam was not good and I was terribly frightened. Still, I believed my husband would come home safely, and I longed for that day.

In such a setting, other people visited me, too, occasionally from nearby churches. Sometimes they came because they were raising money for their buildings or other projects. Others came explaining their belief in God, and claiming that they were the true believers, the real Christians, and that those in other churches were not. They tried to convince me to attend their Bible Study, but I declined their invitations. They reminded me of the king frog in my father's story while I remained the fool frog in the wide world, seeking the King of the whole universe, not just the creator of one small group.

I did become interested in what these different churches believed, however, and began discussing the subject with my neighbors. As one voice concluded, another began, each seeming to have a different opinion:

"I believe in God, but I don't know which church is right, so I don't go at all...."

"The church is a good place to go. They teach you right from wrong, so I go—but I'm not a member...."

"It doesn't matter which church you go to. They all believe in God, so you learn something...."

"Some people say they believe in God and they go to church, but they are hypocrites! I don't go to church anymore," a middle-aged woman said.

"Are you a Christian?" I asked her.

"No, I'm not!" she answered emphatically. I wondered how she could tell the difference between the true Christian and the so-called hypocrite Christian when she wasn't a Christian herself. Who or what are Christians, anyway? What are they made of? I asked myself many questions.

I was confused. I sincerely wanted to know about Christianity, perhaps to become a Christian, but I didn't want to be one of those hypocrites. They sounded like terrible people, though I didn't really understand what the word meant.

As I listened carefully to many voices speaking about God and the Church, I sensed I was getting closer to the place where I would find the answers to my questions: the purpose of my life, and how to help a suffering world. I felt the "eyes to see the truth" were still guiding me, for I believed I wouldn't have come this far already if there were never to be answers to what I desperately wanted to know. At times I trusted these "eyes" completely, not only for myself but for my husband, no matter how bad the news sounded from Saigon.

By the time Tom returned from Vietnam I was thoroughly exhausted, but I felt triumphant that we had both survived the year. Our son was eight months old when my husband held him in his arms for the first time. Gail remembered her Daddy, and her joy when she saw him again was as great as mine. Color and beauty seemed to return to the island as our family was reunited, and we could enjoy our home in the "Paradise of the Pacific" just like everyone else.

Yet it was in this place that I discovered the fragility of human life. Under the pressure of heavy responsibility and the uncertainty of another war, I thought everyone had a built-in longing for eternal life, and for a power beyond themselves. It seemed a natural thing for human beings to

86

seek God, so I didn't think it strange that so many people had their religions and believed in their gods.

After a few happy weeks, I thanked the people of the island for their kindness to the children and me, and wished them happiness in proportion to the great beauty of the island as we prepared to leave for yet another home.

On a bright day in April, 1963, we arrived in Oklahoma for Tom's new military assignment there. As we settled into our rented house near the base, I noticed a small church next door. Before long, I became acquainted with my neighbor, Judy, who was a member of that church. As our friendship grew, Judy and I began discussing deeper subjects, like the world situation and, eventually, God. Although she knew of my Buddhist background, she invited me to go with her to church. I felt completely out of place, but since I didn't want to offend my new friend, and because I did want to learn about this particular church in my attempt to understand them all, I laid aside my discomfort and went with her. Most of what happened there puzzled me for a long time.

One afternoon, while extra meetings they called "revival services" were being held, two men from the church came to visit me. They spoke about God, His Son Jesus, and a lot of things I didn't understand. Finally, they asked me what I believed about God. I told them I believed there was a God who created the whole universe. (I had to be sure we were talking about the same God.) They nodded to each other in silence. I don't think they were too impressed with my answer.

After a long pause, one of the men asked me to bow my head and say the words of a prayer after he said them first. The prayer was about the Son of God, Jesus Christ, who, they said, died on the cross to save the world, and who rose from the grave after three days. By the end of the prayer I had "accepted" this Jesus into my heart. They told me now I would go to heaven when I died.

The men probably thought they had done something wonderful for me, but the only thing I could think of was how selfish I felt. I didn't deserve to be saved before my family was. Was I to go floating up to that wonderful place my grandmother had told me about and leave my husband, my family, his family, and all the friends in Japan who didn't yet know about Jesus? Didn't God remember that the whole purpose of my journey was to find a way to turn the world around, and to bring a taste of heaven down to earth where so many people were suffering? How could I trust a God who cared for me but didn't know my thoughts and desires?

"God cares for everyone, but He wants you to be saved first," one of my visitors said in response to my question. "He does know your heart, and He will save the others, too, one by one, as we pray for them."

I nodded without understanding, feeling that I had to yield to ideas which were beyond mine at this point. The anguish continued, however, for like so many times before, I just didn't know if I were doing the right thing or not. In my prayer I had said, "I accept Jesus Christ," but I didn't have any idea what "accept" meant.

"What if I'm wrong again and don't know it?" I asked the men.

"When you realize you have done something wrong, all you have to do is ask God to forgive you and He will," one of them said softly, as though he were talking to a child.

"He will?" I exclaimed in surprise. If that were true, I thought, then God reminded me of myself, for I had to forgive myself constantly. I could never blame others for my mistakes which, because of my ignorance, I made constantly. Everyday I would make it a practice to forgive myself for the mistakes of the day before. That God would forgive me for all my mistakes, and for everything I did wrong, was amazing to me.

However, without making mistakes or doing anything wrong, I would not have found out the truth about myself in the first place, that I had the capacity to learn, to grow, and to make the right choice. Now I wanted to learn everything I could about this God and His Son, Jesus.

After urging me to attend a church of their denomination wherever we moved next, the two men left. I sat alone in my living room reflecting on all that had happened in such a short time that afternoon. Had I made the right decision today, or ever?

Had I made any progress at all, I wondered—this fool frog on her journey, hopping here and there, stopping to investigate first one possible resting place and then another? No, none, I concluded. I was not only still a fool frog, but a nothing with a load of guilt for supposedly being saved while those I had spent my life trying to help were still hopelessly locked in their suffering.

Once again I retraced the steps of my journey, sick at heart at all the effort I had spent, and the terribly short distance I had traveled. How often I asked the same questions: What does it mean to live? What is life? What is the purpose of my life in this world?

Oh, how I wished for companionship on this journey of mine! Did anyone else ever ask such questions? How could I determine that what I had just done was right? Was I going to keep on trudging, but arrive at the end of my journey with no success at all, and be of no use to anyone?

I cried bitterly, for I sensed the "eyes to see the truth" were watching my heart, and I felt naked and helpless in their presence. I was certain these eyes saw how empty I was, that I was of no value to anyone, and that made me feel very guilty. Had I been wasting my time for all these years?

It was a great disappointment to find nothing of value in

me when I wanted to find something good. Though I had some years of schooling and job training, I didn't feel I was worth anymore now than when I was born. If I had something of value within me, I would be content and satisfied, wouldn't I?

But, my thoughts wavering again, if those "eyes" were real, as I had been convinced so many times they were, then they knew my anguish. Hadn't they brought me to this place for a reason? If they knew I was struggling to become something of value to those I loved, then I wasn't really struggling alone after all, was I?

Though my questions continued, I felt more at peace as I decided to leave my problems to the "eyes" and let them guide me to the place where I could find my solutions. Otherwise, I would always feel guilty about everything I did or didn't do, because I could never discern by myself what was right. I just couldn't change "I don't know" to "I know" by myself, no matter how much I tried. But now I was so completely open to the "eyes" that I felt comfortable enough to depend on them.

Not long after the visit of the two men, Judy gave me a Bible of my own to read. "I know you will be with the Lord someday," she said confidently as she placed the book in my hand.

As I read the first enlightening pages of this Bible, I almost felt exultant. Perhaps I had been led to the truth at last. But before the familiar anguish which seemed to follow every trace of hope along this journey of mine could recur, I retraced my steps again, trying to understand what it was that I feared so much. The answer came quickly: I was afraid of my responsibility for whatever truth I was discovering. What if I made mistakes and thought the wrong answers were the true ones? If I actually found the answers to what I had been seeking for so long, what would I do with them?

And if I found the way to reverse the direction of the world, what was I supposed to do then?

This new burden was giant-sized! The more I thought about it, the more I trembled. For what purpose had I wandered so far, I cried to myself, to the "eyes," to anyone who might be listening anywhere in the universe.

Just then I remembered an incident, a strange incident that had happened in Japan at least ten years before....

One Sunday morning as I was walking down the street near my apartment, thinking about my search as usual, I heard the loud voice of a man very near to me.

"What will you do if you find the answers to your questions?" the voice asked. Immediately I looked around, trying to locate a person to go with the voice, but no one was on the street that quiet Sunday morning except me—not even a stray dog.

Surely, I thought, I heard a voice, but I couldn't find anyone to go with the sound I heard. I stood still for a few moments, trying to understand what had happened. Finally, I dismissed the voice entirely, deciding I must have imagined the whole thing. However, the words I thought I heard from a real man's voice remained with me and created still more questions for my already over-crowded mind: Who will listen to me even if I find the answers I'm looking for? No one, I decided, because I was a woman without any power or higher education, and, in a society where women were supposedly lower than men, I shouldn't be expected to come up with anything to pass along to others anyway.

Still, at that moment, I responded to that real or imaginary voice which had come somehow so clearly to my mind with these words: "I will give the answers I find to the man to whom people will listen!" That seemed like the perfect answer at the time, and I soon forgot the whole incident.

Besides, I reasoned, I couldn't possibly have heard a voice, because there had been no one there. Anyway, why should I worry about that problem now. I had many other bridges to cross first.

Now, more than ten years later, that strange memory surfaced with astonishing reality. My question, "What am I going to do with the answers if I find them?" oppressed me once again and demanded a response. I remembered vividly how helpless I had felt before when I realized I was not someone people would respect or listen to, because I was then only a childish, young woman. And now that I was a full ten years older, I didn't see any change. I was still a woman with almost no education, who would certainly command little respect if I tried to tell people how the universe was run!

But I remembered just as clearly my response to that strange voice: "I will give the answers to a man to whom people will listen!" Who could that man be, I wondered wearily, yet convinced that I had to look now for such a man.

Judy's words returned to me—"I know you will be with the Lord someday"—and I wondered again what she meant. Why was she so confident? The others in her church seemed to understand. Why didn't I? Perhaps the "Lord Jesus" would help me understand, too, or help me find the man people would listen to when I solved the mysteries of life. I also sensed the answers to my questions were in this book called *The Holy Bible*, which everyone in Judy's church seemed to read and believe. Maybe if I started reading this Bible, and going to church, too.... When Tom agreed to go with me, I began to attend church regularly for the first time in my life.

I wish I could say my eyes were suddenly opened, or

that the Bible instantly solved all my spiritual problems, but so much of what I heard in that little church in Oklahoma had nothing to do with my needs. I wanted to understand God more; I wondered about Him all the time. Was He watching me? Did He know about all the churches on earth and all their activities? Why couldn't a sermon or Sunday School lesson satisfy me? Could something be wrong with me? My questions bored deeper and deeper into my heart.

In my dissatisfaction, I often thought of the differences between the two countries I had known, America and Japan, especially their religions. I remembered there were sects and divisions among the followers of Buddha, just as I was learning there were differences among Christians. Some Buddhists, I knew, didn't believe in heaven or hell, life after death, or the judgment, and they opposed those who did. Now I wondered, how both types of people could be Buddhists?

Remembering my Buddhist teachings, I knew we were supposed to be seekers of life in all its love, wisdom, and truth, so I couldn't help but ask the question: Where is truth in all the different sects of Buddhism, in Christianity, and in all other religions of today? Isn't there a truth somewhere that unites them all, binding them all together as one, just as the earth is one? Otherwise, how can it be called truth?

I concluded that many people in the world today had obviously joined the king frog in his small pond, accepting his small knowledge of the truth in exchange for comfort and a sense of security, no matter how fleeting or false.

To discover that Christianity was as divided as Buddhism was a great disappointment for me. I had come from confusion; now I was confused by Christianity. I didn't mind so much being a fool frog still looking for the King of the universe, but I didn't want to keep getting wrong answers, and I didn't want to stay confused forever.

Though I had what Judy and the visitors from the church called the "Word of God" in my own hand, I was afraid to open it for fear it, too, would confuse me even more. Sometimes, however, like a child examining the gift packages under the Christmas tree, I would peek here and there inside its stiff, leather covers, because I was becoming more and more sure that the key to everything I was seeking was in that book. But, for now, it was as though my spiritual eyes were blind, and I needed some assistance before I could unlock its truths. The "eyes to see the truth," who I still believed knew my condition, would have to send someone to teach me how to understand this book.

I sensed my goal was near, near enough to prod me on with my journey toward Christianity or something else in this tossing, turning, 20th-century world. America was experiencing great anguish over the death of its President, John F. Kennedy, and I sympathized as the country expressed her grief. America, who worshiped God openly and freely, who had churches with tall steeples in every town and city and who stamped "In God We Trust" on her coins, now displayed on her faces the familiar, dark shadows of my people during World War II. There was loneliness in the eyes of children, and a thirsty restlessness on the faces of adults.

Oh, how I wanted to know the King of the whole world, the Lord of all creation and all the sad and restless people who lived there, before it was too late!

"Can't you make yourself visible to me?" I cried. "I want to know your thoughts, your purpose for my life, your reason for creating the world." So many unknowns!

But just when I thought I might be close to finding the answers I so desperately sought, Tom received orders of transfer to Germany. Once again I had to switch from my inner journey to an outer one, as my husband went on to his new assignment ahead of us, and I remained behind to pack our belongings and prepare the children and myself to join him there.

The deep, blue sky beckoned me again as I boarded the plane and set my heart toward Germany and another reunion with my husband. It was a relief to set aside the unbearable pressure of my struggle for awhile, even though I knew in my heart that, as I calculated the timing of my inner journey, it was just before dawn. My expectation of a spiritual sunrise grew larger as the last visible speck of American soil faded from view.

The words I had read in snatches from the Bible, the new thoughts I had learned so briefly from those in the little church in Oklahoma, and the tiny beam of awareness about the God of creation who would forgive me for my mistakes, remained in my heart like a carefully stored jewel throughout the long flight....

In the beginning God created the Heaven and the Earth; and the earth was without form and void; and darkness was upon the face of the waters... (Genesis 1:1-2).

I remembered how my heart raced when I read those words at the very beginning of the Bible. Was this the Lord of all creation, the King of the universe of whom my father spoke?

...And the Spirit of God moved upon the face of the waters" (Genesis 1:2).

Again the words I read captured my whole being; the impact was impossible to describe. I recognized the Spirit of God as the One moving upon me, for I was void. The darkness of ignorance was upon the face of my mind. I received the words like a sponge soaks up water, grasping the first hint of understanding how the visible and invisible things of my life touched.

The Bible—something about this strange book seemed familiar. Then I remembered. My aunt had given me a Bible, too—a smaller, older one, when I was about eight years old. I couldn't read it then because it was written in English—my aunt was an English teacher—so I had put it in my bookcase with the other books she gave me just before she died. I never thought I would read the little book, but I had kept it fondly in remembrance of her.

Out of curiosity, soon after Judy gave me the Bible I had now, I compared the two. To my amazement I discovered they were just alike, word for word.

How strange. My aunt, who was Buddhist and probably knew very little about Christianity, was touching me now and, without knowing it, had become another link in the chain of events leading me to the understanding I had sought all my life. Because of my love for her, I had chosen to take English in high school, which enabled me to work on an American Army Base and ultimately meet my husband. If I hadn't learned English, I certainly wouldn't be in America now reading a Bible in the language of the people who lived there. I couldn't deny that some mighty power was working its purpose in my life. It was no longer a question of, "Is there a power?" or, "Are there 'eyes' to see the truth?" I was as positive that those things were real, as I was that I was alive.

But was it the God I had read about in the beginning of the Bible, the One who created the heavens and the earth, who had brought me to this place in my journey? Yes, I agreed, as I finally and joyfully acknowledged the reality of God. Now I wanted to know everything about this God, not only for my sake, but for those who loved me, for those who were searching for Him, too, and for the two women who had given me these two Bibles.

With the surge of joy, however came an accompanying uneasiness as I thought of all my encounters with God, all the way back to my hearing the word "God" for the first time, and knowing that if the word "God" existed, then there had to be something for that word to represent. I heard the word often as I was growing up, but usually in reference to many gods: the god of the village, the god of the well, the god of harvest, the god of fire, the god of business, the god of birth, and *Amaterasu Ohmikami*, the sun goddess of Japan and ancestor of the Emperor, who himself was—until the end of World War II—a god.

Furthermore, there were a number of different religions, each clouded with its accompanying myths or superstitions. People seemed ready to believe anything in times of trouble, I found, yet after the war I remembered many people believed in nothing but themselves. No longer could they believe in the god of Japan who failed to bring them to victory. Still, some people became unbelievably religious in certain new sects of Buddhism, while others clung to the old ways, the teachings of their ancestors, and what they had been taught about their faith.

As I questioned where these religions and superstitions came from, I concluded that they all had their birth in fear. I feared the unknown just as these people did, but none of the religions I heard about satisfied me completely. Somehow, trusting in the love of my people and their way of life, reasoning against the fears that devoured my mind, and racing against time because I knew I might die before I reached my unknown destination, I floundered between all the options I knew as I continued my journey.

Eventually, with so many unknowns, I reached the point where I could only say I was on a journey to an unknown destination, but I was more determined than ever to get there. The Bible, the Word of the God I was learning about, seemed to hold the key to everything I was looking for.

"In the beginning God created the heaven and the Earth...," I pondered again, and the earth where I was, was still without form and void. Darkness was still upon the face of my understanding. Those thoughts mingled with memories of that vivid dream of my childhood when I was awakened, just before dawn, after a long fall through a dark tunnel.

I felt like my life was a slow-motion video of that dream. When the thrilling, sharp lightning revealed where I was after the long fall in the darkness, I was surprised to find myself at the end of an underground tunnel, emerging into the dawning of a stormy, new day. The eastern sky was a visible, light gray. A few trees on the open field were wet and swaying in the strong wind.

As I awoke from the dream, I remember thinking I couldn't have been falling, but I must have been pulled out of the darkness by something. Otherwise, I wouldn't be in that open place under the early morning sky at all, but still underground, buried somewhere in the darkness of the tunnel.

The sky outside my window was dark. My children slept beside me as the plane's engines droned on through the night sky. Although I was hurling through the darkness again, literally, as I sped on my way to Germany, I knew I would soon emerge into the dawn of a new day, and closer to the dawn of my new life. The Word of God I clutched in my hand would show me the way.

Chapter 10
SUNRISE

All too quickly my husband's tour of duty in Germany came to an end, and we had to say *auf wiedersehen* to that lovely country. Even after we moved to Fort Monmouth, New Jersey, and settled into our government housing there, the memories of our life in that European country were as fresh as if we hadn't left.

"What is your religion?" My visitor was surprised that the family he had come to visit no longer lived in our apartment, and his awkward question sounded like an attempt to make up for his mistake.

"I came from a Buddhist family," I replied, "but I believe in God."

"Is that right? Well, I'm Chaplain Johnson, and I serve this housing area. If you ever need me, just give me a call. We welcome you here."

He smiled politely, placed his card in my hand, and turned to go. The polished cross on his collar beamed as he stepped into the morning sunlight that April day in 1968.

The chaplain's visit rekindled the spark that had lain dormant during the three years we spent in Germany, years I spent drinking in the history and culture of that country. Life there was unforgettable: a busy, exciting, joyous time in our lives. We toured the countryside, visited the Alpine regions of Berchtesgaden, Chiemsee, and Garmisch, and witnessed the astonishing beauty of the Rhine River. Their

99

cities were beautiful, too, with such vastly different buildings and gardens from those I had seen in Japan or the United States. There were flowers everywhere—in window boxes, between gas pumps, on cement posts, and across every balcony. I loved walking through the parks and streets, just to absorb their beauty.

But now in our new home, especially after the chaplain's visit, I was thrust back into the life I had known in Oklahoma. The fairyland existence of the intervening three years seemed to float away like a helium-filled balloon whose string has been cut.

The familiar anguish pressed heavily upon me, and I wondered: could this chaplain help me? Had he been sent to me by the power I could sense but had not yet defined? It was strange that he had not been looking for us, but still he had come. I looked at the card in my hand, pronouncing the name, and taking note of the phone number I knew I would soon call.

A few days later Chaplain Johnson came to visit again, not by mistake this time, but in answer to my request. After we greeted each other and he was seated in my living room, however, I didn't know what to say. How could I tell him about my journey, or ask him my questions when I didn't even know what they were myself? And my broken English! I thought he must be sorry he had come to see this foolish, ignorant woman.

Slowly we began to talk, exchanging thoughts about God, the world situation, and the meaning of life. When I was more at ease, I tried to tell him about the "eyes" that followed me, and the pain that pressed me from inside.

He was patient, but I knew he didn't understand what I was trying to tell him, nor could I blame him. My explanation was so poor it didn't even make sense to me. He seemed to be trying hard both to make me feel at ease and to understand what must have been to him a very strange story.

"Why do you think I knocked on your door the first time I came to visit?" he asked quietly.

"Because God sent you," I answered without hesitation.

"What do you think of Buddha now?" he asked.

"I think God made him."

"And what do you think of Christ?"

"He is the exact copy of God in man's form." The answer came out of my mouth instantly, and surprised even me.

Though I didn't know much about God, I tried to explain what I felt He would be like if He came into this human world now. I said I thought He would die of a broken heart because of His love for us and the lack of harmony and love He would find among us. With so much hate and greed in the world, I even wondered if He would stay.

Chaplain Johnson sat thoughtfully on our sofa for a few moments without comment. Then he stood up, went to my bookshelf, and took out the Bible my friend Judy had given me in Oklahoma. Sitting down again, he opened the Bible, underlined some words, and gave me the Bible to read:

For God so loved the world that He gave His only begotten Son, that whosoever believeth in Him should not perish, but have everlasting life (John 3:16).

I easily understood the words printed in red and underlined with the chaplain's blue pen, for I had always felt that, if there is a God, He must love everybody in the world. Otherwise, why did He create flowers, nighttime stars, and the lovely colors of autumn? Isn't it for our eyes to see His beauty and greatness that He placed us here on His beautiful earth? So why did people still fight with each other instead of making that beautiful world a better place for themselves and for others? Why, why, I wondered in my heart! Once again, nothing made sense to me.

"I wish I could see Him now; I need to know so many things," I managed to say. The chaplain was a comfortable person to be with, and I found myself telling him more than I had ever been able to tell another person. I wondered about the time I was taking from his schedule, but he was so patient I kept on:

"I feel I'm the biggest sinner of all," I said. "I don't mind dying if that is what would make the world a better place...."

I paused, unable to make any more words come. Finally, he broke the silence:

"Jesus came to earth once, almost two thousand years ago. He died for all our sins, rose from the grave three days later, and then returned to heaven. But He is coming again."

"Coming again! When?" I had not heard this before.

"Yes, He's coming again. I know that, and He knows that, but no one except God, the Father, knows just when that will be."

For a moment I had been thrilled at the prospect of finally asking my questions directly to Jesus, for I was beginning to feel that He knew the answers to all the questions of the universe. But if no one knew when He was coming, then I was either born two thousand years too late, or who knows how many years too soon.

My mood plummeted again. On the other hand, I felt a gentle gravity pulling me toward this man who exhibited such confidence in what he believed. Why couldn't I be as peaceful as he?

"I don't know why I feel this pain in my heart," I said when the conversation resumed. "I become so depressed when I see the trouble in the world. Why is that?" With the pain stored so long inside me, it felt good to express myself to someone who seemed to understand.

"Everybody feels pain. Truth is pain—to live is pain—to be rich or poor is pain...." This chaplain, who because of his native American heritage must also suffer, spoke as if he were talking to himself. I understood, for he was expressing thoughts I had had for a long time.

"I feel I'm in between all things: between death and life, the visible and the invisible, young and old, good and evil.... Do you ever feel this way?" I asked again.

"Yes, I think everyone feels this way, but I don't have that pain now because I've made my decision for Christ."

I wondered what "decision" he was talking about. I was uncomfortable with the word because I had trouble making any decision on my own. Circumstances usually determined what had to be done, and I just followed through.

"I can't make a decision about anything!" I blurted out. How I wished I were more like the man sitting across from me, who seemed to be totally at peace with whatever he said. I was certain the more we talked, the more I could learn from him about Jesus. Yet I had to realize he was a chaplain, a husband and father who must be very busy, and I shouldn't take up too much of his time. I would have to find another way to learn all I wanted to know, though I doubted there was anyone who had enough time for me, and I was overwhelmed with frustration. But I would ask the chaplain as many questions as I could in the time we were together.

"Do you read the Bible?" He asked, breaking into the silence again.

"Just a little."

"You mean you've never had the experience of reading the Bible to study it?"

"No, not really. I want to, but I'm afraid...."

I could see that my answer puzzled him, but he asked no more questions. After a brief, friendly and quite ordinary chat, he left to return to his office.

For days I couldn't sleep or eat. Each question the chaplain had asked bothered me, and when I compared myself to him, my shortcomings disturbed me greatly. I felt guilty that I had come from a Buddhist family, but lived now in America, a country that stood as "one nation under God." Was I still their enemy?

I didn't know what the chaplain knew, and I didn't have his peaceful view of life. I didn't know what I was, or what I believed. I was somewhere between Buddhism and Christianity, between the known and unknown, walking on this tightrope called life. I pictured myself maneuvering between the sharp blades of differing human societies, trying not to hurt anyone, and I was doing all this so I might find the true way of life for myself and everyone else. Yet compared to someone like the chaplain, I felt almost like I was something evil.

I began to wonder what Christians think of Buddhists, and how I appeared to them. Though I loved both Americans and the people of my own background, I began to feel unwelcome here. Buddha taught us to be peacemakers, to love, to forgive, and not to harm any living thing, and all these teachings made sense to me. What didn't make sense was that no one seemed to pay much attention to that kind of life. That's why my suffering existed, trying to figure out why that was true. I loved Buddha and respected him. I believed he loved me, too. Otherwise, why did he spend his entire lifetime searching for those things and teaching them to all human beings?

But, I remembered, even under the umbrella of Buddhism, not everyone believed the same things. Some even believed there was no heaven and hell. So, I wondered,

104

how could they call themselves Buddhists? The key to understanding Buddhism was to know the heart of Buddha, I thought.

I reasoned continually, trying to find the way forward on my inner journey, but no peace came. I was at the end of my being. I had used myself all up.

During my desperation I thought often of the chaplain and longed to talk with him again, even though, just as often, I feared I would be a bother to him. Finally I dialed his number anyway, because I had to speak to someone who knew God. Though it was evening, he came without complaint. I'll never forget his kindness.

"I feel I'm evil and I don't know why," I began emotionally.

"Why do you think such a thing?" he scolded tenderly.

"...and I don't know who I am. I seem to lose my identity, and I don't know the reason for that, either," I sobbed.

He was silent for a long time before continuing in the same, gentle tone he had used before:

"*Chiga*—such a beautiful name. What does it mean?" I knew he was trying to cheer me up by changing to a lighter subject.

"It means a thousand or eternal blessings, or a thousand or eternal celebrations of undefiled newness."

As I explained my name to the chaplain, I felt guilty again because I hadn't lived up to the expectation of my family. I had been told I was named "Chiga" because I was born in the month of our New Year celebration. The chaplain's question brought me back to the origin of my birth, and I saw the reason I felt I had lost my identity. I didn't deserve the name I had been given. Now I really felt like a nobody—no name, just a body made of dust.

"How beautiful," the chaplain said again, interrupting my negative thoughts. "Your parents must have been so proud at your birth." He made no mention of my obvious sadness.

Suddenly, as we talked, I noticed a light coming from his chest area. All my senses were roused by the strange sight before me, and I wondered if I were awake or asleep. I rubbed my eyes to be sure. He noticed my changed expression.

"What is it?" he asked, looking down at his chest. "Do you see a light or something?"

"Yes, I saw a light." But then it was gone and I couldn't see it anymore.

The chaplain smiled, acting as though the incident were unimportant. He continued the conversation, asking me about Japan and my family, all in an effort to cheer me up, I thought. I was surprised that he made no further reference to the light. His concern for me was touching.

"You are very tired and, perhaps, you are homesick, too. Would you like to go home for awhile to see your family? If you do, I'll try to have your husband reassigned to Japan. I can't guarantee I'll be successful, but I can try."

He studied my face for my reaction. I knew he was sincere.

"That would be nice, but I don't want you to go through all that trouble for me."

"It's no trouble," he said. "Chaplains often recommend reassignment when, in their judgment, a soldier or the family would benefit from it."

I was grateful for his offer, and for his concern for me, but I knew the reassignment would not come through for us. I also knew that my anguish was not from homesickness, but from my inability to find answers to my relentless questions, and from the constant frustration of maintaining a balance between my journey as a woman with a family, and a human being born into circumstances such as mine. I knew it wouldn't help to go home, but the chaplain's kindness was precious and I appreciated his offer to try.

106

"Well, then. I'll let you know when the papers come back." His eyes smiled, but I detected worry on his face as he stood up to go. I thanked him for coming, though I still felt unworthy of his kindness.

For the next few weeks I managed to concentrate on my children and housework, but I was never free of anguish. I had no idea how to move from that stagnant spot.

Tom was frantic. I'd hardly eaten or slept for weeks. He didn't know what to do for me because I couldn't explain what was wrong. Everything was a mystery to us both. Now I felt guilty for making everyone else worry about me. My senses were slowly dying to the outside world, and I seemed to drift away from reality. I thought I shouldn't keep on living this way, making everyone unhappy, even though I never intended to do that.

I thought of divorcing so I could go away and bear my anguish alone, setting my husband free from the agony I had created for him. I thought of killing myself, too, so I could truly end my journey, but I couldn't do that because I loved my family and those who had cared for me throughout my life. I saw no way out but to stay here and cling to life the best way I could.

At some point during this time, memories of things I didn't understand about my father and grandfather when I was so young, now began to make sense to me....

My grandfather—he who left nothing behind, who didn't cling to the things of the world, always seemed to be climbing a mountain. As my grandmother would say, "Your grandfather could see the other side of the mountain." Now I understood: the mountain is called "suffering," and there is another side.

My father—he who identified with the fool frog, who was in search of the King of the world, seemed to be taking his place beside me in my journey. I was too small to know much about him during his lifetime, but after his death I

107

learned he suffered greatly because he didn't believe in the Japanese god, nor agree with the military government. He opposed the war and was ostracized by his fellow workers. The blindness of the Japanese people saddened him deeply, because he loved his country and its people very much.

Now, it seemed to me, if I were destined to walk this path, to continue the journey my father and grandfather began, and if I quit before I finished that journey, was there anyone else to take my place? No one, I concluded.

Just then I had a new thought. Something seemed familiar. I'd felt this way before—in my dream, when I was falling in the darkness, not knowing where I would land. Then lightning flashed and I saw the dawning sky above my head and trees swaying in an open field. That time I had awakened, relieved that I had only been dreaming. Even in the dream, without the lightning I wouldn't have known where I was, and I remembered the terror of being in the darkness forever. How beautiful and refreshing that open field had been.

Now, on my inner journey, I had come to a place where I couldn't move in any direction. I was tired, drained, without energy to go on, and I wasn't dreaming. Yet, faintly, I sensed that, as in my dream, dawn would eventually come.

The dream and my current condition were so similar. In both I seemed to be drifting endlessly in the darkness, and in neither did I know where I was or where I would end up. Now, just as the lightning flashes revealed my exact location and ended my nightmare, I wished the light which shone from the chaplain's chest would bring an end to the daily nightmare of my life. How I wanted this dark, nighttime journey to end.

I thought again about my father's frog story, the incident which had launched my journey in the first place. The story didn't come to a conclusion, but I who had identified with the fool frog all my life, felt responsible to find the King of the whole world anyway, just in case my father wanted me to. I shouldn't give up, I told myself, just because things sometimes got scary and mysterious.

Maybe I was sick, or losing my mind. The people around me must have thought that, anyway. Still, I wanted to talk with Chaplain Johnson at least once more, if only to tell him about my dream and the lightning that revealed where I was. I wanted to see if he thought there was any connection between the lightning and the light I had seen from his chest. It didn't seem logical that the second light had appeared to me without a reason.

I thought it would be easy to tell him my unusual story, but just like the first time he came to visit, I didn't know where to begin. In my desperation I dissolved into sobs and simply cried out to him to save me.

Similar to the men in Oklahoma, Chaplain Johnson quietly but firmly guided me through a prayer, his words which I repeated after him. Then he prayed fervently that my spiritual condition would be healed.

Immediately I felt unburdened, not because I was saved (I still couldn't grasp that concept), but because his kindness and concern were so sincere. I didn't feel that my problems were solved, but I felt I could trust this man to teach me about the Bible and help me find my way out of the quandary I had been in for so long.

But before I could voice my desire that he be my teacher, he announced in a tone I had never heard him use before: "I must go to Vietnam. Another chaplain will come to take my place. And now, about the person of the Holy Spirit...." he said in a strict, official tone, and he began to explain some of the words he had used in his prayer.

"I think I know," I heard myself saying, even though I didn't have any idea what he intended to tell me. But at that moment I knew I was in the presence of the "eyes to see the truth," and the thought came to me that the owner of the "eyes" was the Holy Spirit, the present-day form of God. Neither one had a body that I could see—I didn't even know if either one was a person. All the details seemed to be veiled from my own eyes and from my understanding.

But in the days that followed, I continued to fluctuate back and forth between thinking I was near the end of my journey, and asking the same, old questions like a dissatisfied child, and my condition didn't improve. Because I was so weak physically, I decided to admit myself to the hospital to regain my strength, at least enough to cope with my housework and children.

Almost as soon as I entered the mental hospital, I felt my anguish removed. With the aid of medication I slept like a baby, ate and enjoyed my food, and felt better than I had in months. Before long I began noticing other patients, and I found myself responding automatically to their needs. I talked, listened, and laughed with them. It felt good to be alive, to help others, to be useful again.

Somehow I realized that I was helping them, and as I concentrated more on the needs of others, my own pain diminished and I was being healed myself. The hint of an idea occurred to me, that perhaps the God I was beginning to know wanted me to use my life to help others find solutions to their problems, just as I was nearing the answers to my own.

While I was in the hospital, our former President's brother, Robert Kennedy, was shot and killed during his own presidential campaign. The day I heard the news I awakened to the world outside the hospital where all kinds of sickness occur just like on the inside. Anger at the killing, such as I never knew existed, suddenly flared within me like a summer tempest. Not knowing how to direct this anger, I groaned in despair for the whole human race.

But the anger was a stepping stone, driving me back to my journey, and channeling my thinking again toward the Bible. My thirst to know the King of the whole world was overpowering, and I couldn't wait any longer for someone to come and teach me how to read this book. Right then I realized that the fear of making a mistake had kept me from reading the Bible anyway. This fear had become my excuse not to study alone, but to depend on someone else to teach me the things I thought I couldn't learn by myself.

"Oh, well," I boldly said to myself. "If I make mistakes, if I go in the wrong direction and end up in the small pond, so be it!" Courage to begin meeting my own needs slowly rose from inside me and began to replace my fear. Besides, I chuckled, I was already a fool, a nothing, a sinner full of guilt, a person made of dust. What more could I lose?

In that simple decision which, I would realize later I made by myself, the fear that had gripped me for so long was gone. I felt free now to open up the Bible, to read, to study, and to find the answers I had sought with all my being for so long. I must depend on the "eyes to see the truth" about this too, I said to myself.

My doctor was very kind to me. When I told him I wanted to go home, he replied thoughtfully, almost lovingly: "You were very tired. I can see that you work very hard, and I think you are all right now. But why don't you stay another week just to rest. This is your vacation. You went deep into your spirit, beyond yourself, farther than even a psychologist would go."

I smiled, accepting his kindness and agreeing to his suggestion. I also thought about his words, "beyond yourself." Did I really do that? No wonder no one could help me!

Tom and the children came often to visit me, and we played together on the hospital lawn or took walks around the well-kept grounds. Chaplain Johnson visited me, too, even though he was busy preparing for Vietnam. I was loved by so many, and I loved them all in return. I hoped someday I would be able to repay the kindness and love they gave to me, though, at that moment, I didn't think I could possibly repay them all.

The hospital staff was happy about my quick recovery. They became my friends, too, during our three weeks together. I enjoyed walking outside the hospital buildings and under the trees with their comfortable shade and cooling breezes. Sunshine sparkled across the green, summer lawn; birds sang their accompaniment to the tranquility; and squirrels scampered about, adding comedy and life to my surroundings. I rested well.

Not long after I arrived home from the hospital, Chaplain Johnson came with the news that our request for reassignment to Japan had not been approved, but I knew that from the beginning. He seemed disappointed that he had failed me, but he was happy to see me recovered. I thanked him for his efforts, noticing that he seemed tired in his own journey in life. Preparations to leave were no doubt reducing his energy and enthusiasm.

How I hated to see him leave, to spend a year in that war-torn country as my husband had done. But I was confident he would return just as Tom did. He called once again before he left, saying good-bye and telling me to take care of myself and be a good mother. He reminded me of my brother.

Why this war? Why any war? Isn't there a wisdom somewhere to solve such a terrible problem? Many kings in many ponds all across the earth seemed to be displaying their power, and the only result was to bring each other pain. Though the news was full of talks of peace, there was no peace, and I wondered where the world was heading. For this reason, too, I was determined to find the King of the whole world. He had to have the wisdom I sought!

My life was suddenly very full. I needed to take driving lessons, go to chapel regularly, and meet my family's needs. The days and weeks flew by.

One evening, without any particular forethought, I turned on the TV and heard a man speaking. His strong, forceful words caught my attention. In the background above his head hung a large banner with the words, "Jesus said, 'I am the way, the truth, and the life.'"

The way? The truth? The life? Aren't those the things I've been looking for all my life? Then it was Jesus I had been searching for. But He's not here to speak to me, and the chaplain had said no one knew when He would come back to earth. Is there another way to know Him and talk to Him now?"

I listened intently, hearing this man speak about the world condition, about the signs of the times, and the coming judgment. He mentioned someone named Noah, a story that was not familiar to me, but I was struck that, like the chaplain, here was another man who knew much about God, and he was confident about what he believed, just as the chaplain was.

I learned that the man's name was Billy Graham. I had no doubt that this man loved America, the world, and all its people. He understood the condition of the world, too, knew that it was abnormal and sickly, and he presented that needy world a solution: the person of Jesus Christ, its Savior and Lord.

With a shaky hand and in my broken English, I wrote to Billy Graham, after noting the address which flashed on my screen at the end of the program. I told Mr. Graham how much his speech had helped me.

Then I opened my Bible to the beginning of the Gospel of John. I read from the beginning of the first chapter to the place where the chaplain had underlined in chapter 3:

In the beginning was the Word, and the Word was with God, and the Word was God. The same was in the beginning with God. All things were made by Him, and without Him was not anything made that was made....

Every word revealed God to me, and suddenly I felt I had known Him for a long time. I thought back so long ago to my childhood, when I had first heard the word "God," and felt there must be a thing or a person to go with the word. What kind of heart does He have, I wondered, to make the flowers with their many shapes, colors, and smells? What kind of mind would create the deep, blue sky and decorate it with countless stars at night? These words, telling me that this God had created everything, penetrated my heart in a way nothing had ever done before.

Whether I understood the words or not, between chores, caring for my family, and my other activities, I continued to read the Bible. Often I read until I couldn't read anymore, overwhelmed by this God who had been revealed to mankind in the form of Jesus Christ. I was right; He was the perfect copy of God in man's form! And, when I learned that one of the meanings for the name Jesus was, "God with us," I was stunned, for God was in the very name, Jesus.

I could hardly stand the impact of learning how much God cared for the world and for me. Tears flooded my eyes like a river as I understood for the first time the meaning of prayer, and the meaning of "accept" which the men in Oklahoma and Chaplain Johnson had used in their prayers with me. My constant pain slowly began to change to an indescribable, deep joy, which nothing could take away from me.

This understanding didn't come instantly, but the words I read began to unveil so many things I hadn't understood about life before. Eventually, as Jesus began to make himself known to me more and more personally, I clearly and positively acknowledged Him as my own Savior.

Through a Bible study course I received from Billy Graham, and my daily reading, I grew in my knowledge and understanding of Jesus Christ. To me, He was the sun, rising in glorious splendor in the midst of my being, pushing darkness and its nightmares away forever, and never to set again. He was my Lord, my Savior, and the King who delivered me out of darkness, out of the womb of this world, and into his Kingdom. I had come to know my Father in heaven, the giver of eternal life through His Son. No longer was I just a person of dust, a nobody. I was a child of God, chosen by Him, cleansed of my sins by Him, and able to live forever with Him in that heaven I had longed for all my life.

When I could see God's creative hands forming, not just the earth, but someone like me, I recognized Him as my creator. For now I knew that those many years of anguish, fear, and guilt along the way of my journey were His molding fingers to make me the person He wanted me to be. I realized His revelation of Himself to me came just at the right time, when I could absorb this knowledge and be ready to receive Him—not before, and not when it might have been too late. I was amazed at His perfect timing, and all I could say was, "Thank you, Father!" He knew everything about me now, and He always had.

On December 7, 1969, after our family had spent much time with another chaplain studying the Bible, Tom and I and our two children were baptized together, becoming Christians publicly for the first time. We acknowledged that Jesus was our Savior and Lord, the One who had died in our place and given us a new birth by His resurrection power.

Yes, I had learned, we were created for the pleasure of our heavenly Father and for His glory, just as our children had brought so much joy to us.

Finally, I was at the sunrise of my life. My day had begun.

Chapter 11
REFLECTION

Dark, ominous clouds filled the sky outside my classroom window.

"The typhoon is approaching more quickly than predicted," our teacher said, her voice mounting with tension. "You must leave immediately for home!"

Trees behind the school swayed like ocean waves in the strong wind as we third-graders hurriedly followed our teacher's instructions. Rain would pour from the sky at any moment. We started to run.

By the time my group reached the small river near our home, rain was coming down in torrents. Within minutes dirty, red water swirled over the river's banks, covering the familiar footbridge and temporarily halting our journey home.

Just then we saw several men running down the hill across the river toward us. Even with the poor visibility, I recognized my father among them. I saw him cup his hands around his mouth and shout something to me, but his voice was drowned out by the roar of the river, the pounding rain, and the wind.

Desperate to hear what he was saying, I lunged into the rolling water toward him. Instantly my pace slowed. I fought against the water, stumbled across huge rocks lodged on the floor of the bridge, and shielded myself from floating debris as the angry water surged downstream. I had taken only a few steps when the water splashed high above my waist. I stopped in terror.

When I dared to look up, I saw my father's hand stretched out toward me. And I saw something else: all the other fathers were following him. All those fathers suddenly reminded me of my friends, and I turned to see where they were. I was astonished to find all the other children right behind me. They had followed me into the water, too!

I panicked. I didn't mean to lead the others into the river, but they had followed me anyway. The responsibility was overwhelming, but I knew we had to do something fast. We quickly held hands to fortify ourselves against the strong current, and together took careful steps toward our fathers. When we were midway across the bridge we dropped each other's hands and grasped the strong, steady hands of our fathers. We felt as safe then as if we were already home.

The typhoon incident stretched before me like a vision as I read the following words: "And other sheep I have which are not of this fold; them also *I must bring, and they shall hear my voice*; and there shall be one fold and one shepherd" (John 10:16).

How many incidents had there been in my life to save me from danger, to bring me to the end of my journey to Jesus, my Savior, my shepherd? Would I have been able to take that journey without my grandfather's example, without my grandmother's religious teachings, or my father's frog story? Without my mother's decision to let me leave home, and her blessing when I left my country? Would I have continued my search if I had not chosen English as a course in school, or had a desire to change the world after the war? Would I even be alive if the gentle, old man hadn't caught me when I fell from the persimmon tree? Without any of these people, these events, or "saviors," perhaps I wouldn't have come to the place where I finally met the

Savior of the world, and learned that I was one of the sheep for whom He would comb the world and give His life.

I remembered how it felt when I reached across that terrifying water for my father's hand. I thought he would scold me for my foolish actions, but he didn't say a word. He just gripped my hand in his and smiled at me with his loving eyes, still visible though his face was covered with rivulets of rain.

My journey into the unknown had been like that. Just as I obeyed my instincts to step into that water, just as I was buffeted by the current and unsure of my way during the typhoon, my inner journey had been forged in ignorance and troubled by uncertainty and storms. But when I thought I couldn't move forward anymore, when I had come to the end of myself, I met my oncoming Savior. When I learned the lovely story of His great love for me, and stretched my hand out to be clasped in His, He led me to the safety of His kingdom. I thought He, too, would punish me for my foolishness, but I learned instead that He took my punishment on Himself, and set me free from any penalty at all for my sins. And like my earthly father, after saving me, He walked beside me to guide my unsteady steps.

I talked to Jesus constantly, for I believed He understood everything about me, and could answer all my questions:

"Oh, please forgive me," I would say. There was so much I didn't know, like thinking it was I who had to save the world from going to hell. "Please forgive the world, too," I would add, "for they are ignorant of you just as I was. Thank you for making yourself visible to me. Now I know you, but how can I tell the world about your goodness and your love? No one will listen to me, as you know...."

Many things had happened along my journey which I couldn't explain, but I know now it was Jesus who was behind all those mysteries—even my dream about falling through the tunnel, hearing the loud voice, the similarity between the dream and my journey, and the light from the chaplain's chest.

Now I understood that the One who said, "I am the light of the world" (John 8:12); "the narrow door" (Luke 13:24, NIV); "the bread from heaven" (John 6:41); "the good shepherd" (John 10:11); and "the way, the truth, and the life" (John 14:6) was using any means possible to reveal Himself to me through my stubborn, clouded mind. The richness of His wisdom, His knowledge, and His power as "Creator of heaven and earth" (Genesis 14:19, NIV) and "author of life" (Acts 3:15, NIV)—all those things worked together for the good purpose He had for me (see Romans 8:28).

My impossible journey past the visible into the invisible, my pilgrimage to discern the truth of both worlds, reached fulfillment when I read:

In the beginning was the Word, and the Word was with God, and the Word was God. The same was in the beginning with God. All things were made by Him, and without Him was not anything made that was made (John 1:1-3).

Just as I thought! There was a word, "God," so there was a real God. All His creation has names and words to describe them. Finally, because of this Creator God, who came to earth in human form in the person of Jesus Christ to show his love for all mankind, my lifelong struggle made sense to me.

As I continued studying the Bible I learned many more words about this real God, including those He spoke Himself:

My thoughts, says the Lord, are not like yours, and my ways are different from yours. As high as the heavens

are above the earth, so high are my ways and
thoughts above yours. My word is like the snow and
the rain that come down from the sky to water the
earth. They make the crops grow and provide seed for
planting, and food to eat. So also will be the word that
I speak. It will not fail to do what I plan for it; it will
do everything I send it to do (Isaiah 55:8-11, GNB).

These words were like rain from above, soaking my being with warm memories of my loved ones. Although my family were Buddhists, what they had taught me and how they lived often touched my life with an unforgettable warmth. Now I could relate their example to what I was reading in the Bible.

I thought of my grandmother's teaching about heaven and hell, of judgment and life after death, and her strong emphasis on forgiveness and being kind to others. I was stunned when I read Proverbs 24:16-17: "For a just man falleth seven times and riseth up again, but the wicked shall fall into mischief." This verse reminded me of her telling us children: "Even when you fall seven times you must get up for the eighth time. That's the Buddhist Spirit!" As a child I often fell and scraped my knees, and she would say those very words to encourage me to get up by myself.

The Bible attracted me even more when I thought of the family I had left behind, especially the anguish of cutting the relationship further by becoming a Christian. I wondered if Buddha had received wisdom from God, if the Enlightener who had taught him was the Word of God, our Lord Jesus Christ. When I continued to read the first chapter of John, the Bible answered still another question for me: "That was the true light which lighteth every man that cometh into the world," (John 1:9). I was positive now that Christ had given spiritual understanding to Buddha, even if it was only in part.

I didn't know it then, but that assurance about the connection between Buddha and God's wisdom would sustain me when I encountered an unexpected challenge to my new-found faith.

In 1969 Tom received orders again, this time for an unaccompanied tour to Korea, and the children and I moved into Waiting Wives' Quarters near Fort Riley in Salina, Kansas. One Sunday evening, not long after we arrived, I was invited to attend a new church. Eager to learn more about Christianity, I looked forward to going.

"Buddhism is satanic!" the young speaker said, raising his authoritative voice. Since I was the only person of Oriental descent in the congregation, I knew his words were addressed to me.

His voice pierced my heart. Once again I felt the familiar anguish of the past when I didn't know what was true and what was false. I went home pondering what he meant by the word, "satanic."

The American College Dictionary on my shelf defined Satan as "the chief evil spirit; the great adversary of man; the devil."[1] Another reference, *The Handy Dictionary of the Bible* had these definitions of Satan: "adversary, chief of the fallen spirits, devil, accuser of the brethren, the old serpent, evil one, murderer, the prince of this world, the great dragon,"[2] and more.

Whatever definition I came up with increased my anguish. After all I had experienced, after all I had learned, how could I accept the word, "satan," as the definition of a teaching and a people I loved so much?

I remembered that my grandmother had said during my childhood: "Don't walk in the way of the serpent." Why would she tell me that if Buddha—*Shaka*—which means "Enlightened one"—whom she told me to follow, was the

[1] *New York: Random House,* 1963-64, p.1078.
[2] *Michigan: Zondervan Publishing House,*1965-73, p.134.

122

same as the serpent? Was my grandmother wrong, or was the fault with this Christian speaker?

Perhaps, I thought, Buddhism is not fully understood, that only its superstition and tradition are known. Besides, as I learned when I grew older, Buddhism is so divided by its followers, by those who oppose each other in their teachings and beliefs, that the truth is often lost in the process.

Though I still didn't understand everything about Buddhism or Christianity, I had felt this quandary in both religions, for Christianity, too, seemed to flounder sometimes in confusion and division. There was still plenty of darkness on the earth, I decided, no matter where in the world we are, or what we say we believe.

This had been the reason for my journey, to sort out this confusion, to add light to the misunderstandings we have of each other. When knowledge is incomplete, I found, people accuse one another of terrible and untrue things. I am certain that the serpent is alive, well-fed by all our ignorances, and cleverly trying to deceive and confuse us all.

But I have learned that the Creator, who is also our provider, sustainer, and enlightener, searches the hearts and understands the desires of those who seek Him. He will make Himself known to anyone who hungers to know the true meaning of life, and longs to know His purpose for them. I thought back to my own experience as a child exploring the beauty of nature around me, and wondering who made all those things. But now, as I read the following words, I knew God was revealing Himself to me even then: "Ever since God created the world, His invisible qualities, both His eternal power and His divine nature have been clearly seen. Men can perceive them in the things that God has made" (Romans 1:20, TEV).

Because we lack "the eyes to see the truth," we have difficulty experiencing His presence. Often the way to God is blocked by fear, pride, or even by religion. Actually, He is very near, but because of His invisibility, our ignorance, and our unbelief, His presence seems far away. And, oh, how faithfully we choose to follow our own traditions instead of clinging to His voice of truth! How convincingly we follow our feelings rather than the Word and Spirit of God.

It took such a long time for me to break through layer after layer of man-made knowledge to discern the truth. Many reject Jesus because they are too attached to the tangible, visible things they already know. This is how Satan, the deceiver, easily possesses strongholds in our lives, our governments, and even our churches. If I had retained the traditions of Buddhism, I would still not know the true Enlightener.

How many Buddhists seek real truth in these chaotic days? How many Christians walk in the truth they have been taught, displayed in Christ and His Word? From these questions, it seems that what we believe is not always the complete truth, but only a portion. Satan may deceive us, but Jesus exposes his lies, and informs our ignorance, by the light of His truth. That is why He had to come to earth, and why God also gave us the written Word, so we could be corrected when we were wrong. God, who knows the beginning and the end of all our lives, is always one step ahead of us. His thoughts and ways are always higher than ours, but He and His Word are always with us to reveal those thoughts and ways, replacing ours with His.

Throughout my journey to seek the truth, light (in both its physical and symbolic forms) had played an important role. But, I realized now, this idea was nothing new to me. As a student of Buddhism, I was taught that the way to seek the truth was to blow out my own light when I came in contact with a light that was bigger than mine. This teaching made sense to me at the time, and I further learned, enlightenment

124

according to Buddha is a life of self-denial and respecting others above oneself. In Christ, the greater light, this is called the way of the cross, the path to a enlightenment in this dark world.

Like my small light, if something is true only for my own family but doesn't apply to my neighbor, then that light is not large enough and it cannot be called the truth. When I realized that Christ, who died and rose again from the dead, was the true and great light, that He was large enough to shine throughout the whole world, the light I was brought up under wasn't big enough anymore.

However, Buddhism may still be considered a light—much like moonlight—which, while it may shed some light on our path during the nighttime hours, could never compare to, nor take the place of, the sun. During the day, the Son of God, the true light of the world, has been revealed to us, out-shining all else. As the Word of God continued to unveil its truth to me, the scales dropped like opened shades from my eyes. I no longer wondered which religion was right, Buddhism or Christianity, and I began to understand so much:

And God said, "Let there be light," and there was light. And God saw that the light was good: and God divided the light from the darkness. And God called the light, "day," and the darkness He called "night." And the evening and the morning were the first day (Genesis 1:3-5).

And God made two great lights; the greater light to rule the day, and the lesser light to rule the night. He made the stars also. And God set them in the firma-ment of the heaven to give light upon the earth, and to rule over the day and over the night, and to divide the light from the darkness: and God saw that it was good (Genesis 1:16-18).

The creation story seemed to tell me that, behind the visible day and night, an invisible dimension to the world exists. This dimension is the spiritual "day" and "night," which was created when God called the light into position by His spoken Word (Genesis 1:3-5) even before He set the visible lights in the sky (v. 16-18). "Let us make man in our image," He said in Gen. 1:26, thereby giving us the ability to understand spiritual realities as well as physical ones. This truth also appears in the New Testament, in John's Gospel: "In Him (Jesus) was life, and that life was the light of men" (John 1:4), and when the Apostle Paul encountered Jesus in the "great light" that halted his journey on the road to Damascus (Acts 9:3-6).

Now I understood why I always felt that what I was taught in my childhood was very much like what I was learning about Christianity. Why, then, can't we compare the commonalities of the two religions, instead of looking at each other like enemies. To Christians, Buddhism may appear to be satanic, but the truth is, Jesus wants to reconcile all mankind to Himself—including Buddhists. He can use what Buddhists already know, and direct them into the fullness of His truth.

Buddhists are like those who live in the nighttime, and who, to the extent of their understanding, repent of their sins by following the teachings of Buddha. I believe Buddha was created in the midst of fallen men by the mercy of God to sustain those who were searching for truth in what to believe, and guidance in how they should conduct their lives in harmony with others and creation.

Therefore, according to my understanding, Buddha functioned as a spiritual moon to illumine the spiritual night, but that light could not have fulfilled its purpose unless, like the physical moon, it had a source from which to receive its light. Just as the physical moon receives its light from the sun, so Buddha received his spiritual light from Jesus, the Son of God. As the light of the moon shines from night to morning, so the teaching of Buddha will sustain his followers in his light—until the greater light (the source of Buddha's enlightenment) appears.

They will not be disappointed to know Christ, the greater light. For greater knowledge (light) contains the lesser knowledge (light) within. They will also gain additional knowledge of the Enlightener Himself, who is the Word of God, the Creator of all.

It was the responsibility of Christ, who gave light to Buddha to complete Buddha's faith for his followers, so he came to claim them by His Gospel, and enlighten them with greater light. It is a fulfillment of His Word:

> *And other sheep I have which are not of this fold; them also* I [Jesus] must bring, *and* they shall hear my voice; *and there shall be one fold, and one shepherd* (John 10:16, emphasis added).

Praise God who came to display the way of love! Now I understand why I couldn't let go of this subject that had consumed me for so long. Despite my anguish, it was God's will to call me out of my people and introduce me to His Word so I would know who He was, and what His purpose was for me and for other Buddhists. He who always stands behind what He says, fulfilled His Word to me.

Because I had so many questions, He met my need by quenching my thirst for the truth, and by making Himself known to me. Through His Word, He answered my questions so clearly that He had my full attention: the "eyes to see the truth," the real God to go with the Word, the many references to the "light," and eventually the words, "I am the way, the truth, and the life...." If He hadn't held onto me so tight, if He hadn't raised all those questions in my heart which He would also eventually answer, I would have given up my search and gone "the way of the world" long ago.

Now I could see that the object of my people's belief was to be faithful to those who had given that belief to them. They accepted what they were taught because it made sense to them, and then passed it on to me. I even understood why they taught me to honor our ancestors, and to respect and love our children: it was to keep the family united beyond death. This was how their belief had been kept alive through the years—their very lives had hung on what they believed.

To my people, Buddhism was like a pipeline of faith extending from generation to generation. They were on a journey, too—traveling at night, guided by the moonlight, and believing, because of their faith, they would go to heaven when they died. I believe now that their teaching of "judgment after death" points to the judgment of God.

When Jesus said, "I am the way, the truth, and the life: no man cometh unto the Father, but by me" (John 14:6), He was speaking about His dying on the cross in our place, taking on Himself the judgment that would have been pronounced on us. Christ our Advocate presented the Father His suffering in the place of our sins, pleading mercy for us. The day the faithful followers of Buddha reach the truth of Jesus Christ, their faith will be complete.

My people didn't know it was Christ who died for them, but they believed in a judgment, and in a prosecutor called *Enma*, the judge from hell who would seek punishment for their sins when they died. (I know now that, in the English language, *Enma* is called Satan.) My people expected to escape hell and go to heaven by the extent to which they applied their faith to their lives, like my grandmother's strong emphasis on forgiveness.

Whatever they thought, or didn't understand, I believe that Jesus knows every heart that accepts His words and responds to them. I thank Him for dying for every person, everywhere, in every generation, who follows the path of truth that eventually leads to Him.

As I continue thinking about this Savior of the whole world, I treasure His mysterious works, His unlimited love, and His power to gather His own from all nations and all religious faiths into one fold, with Himself as their shepherd. I don't understand all of this, but neither did the disciples. Jesus tried to explain it to them, and to us:

Jesus then said to His disciples, "I assure you: it will be very hard for rich people to enter the Kingdom of heaven. I repeat: it is much harder for a rich person to enter the kingdom of God than for a camel to go through the eye of a needle." When the disciples heard this, they were completely amazed. "Who, then, can be saved," they asked. Jesus looked straight at them and answered,"This is impossible for man, but for God, everything is possible" (Matthew 19:23-26, GNB).

How true it is! Men and women who trust their riches always find it difficult to know Him or to enter into His Kingdom, when He made it so easy for us. All we have to do is believe Him, accept His Word by faith, and follow Him to do His will. He has accomplished everything else for us. He has done what none of us could have achieved by ourselves. All man-made religions are human efforts to express what they believe, but the Gospel of Christ is what God has done, is doing, and will do for all mankind. Today, I humbly acknowledge that my impossible journey was made possible by Jesus Christ, my Lord, for with God, everything is possible, indeed. I thank Him for His act of grace forever!

I was delighted when I discovered that the Lord of Creation became a human being like me, and lived on the same earth I do. When I think of His earthly ministry, I like to call it heaven on earth, which was another of my desires so long ago. I remembered when my grandmother first told me about heaven and I thought, rather than go there myself, I wanted to bring heaven down to earth—which seemed possible to me. So once again, I learned that a task I thought was up to me had already been accomplished by my Lord. He not only came to take away the sins of the world, dispel what is false, and reveal what is true, but He brought a taste of heaven with Him. What courage, love, and wisdom He displayed!

Each discovery about Jesus stunned me. He died to take away the sins of the world, the sins of my people, my sins—everyone's—and He paid that price centuries before I knew about it. Jesus came to enlighten the people of all nationalities and religions, so that the world might become one in Him and have the kind of peace that is only possible with God. How sad that so much of the world has chosen to reject that wonderful offer, and to miss out on all that love and peace.

I could see from my painful experience that no religion could be complete without the "author and finisher of our faith" (Hebrews 12:2), for all religion is born in the hearts of men who, throughout history, have sought the reason for their existence, and the hope of a better life beyond this world. We call these "earthly religions," because they had their origin in men or women who didn't know the Enlightener, the giver of all truth, themselves. But the Enlightener knew those to whom he had given a portion of truth. The amount of that truth was determined by the quality and openness of their hearts.

One day this true Enlightener, the Author of life, became a man and came to earth to complete what He had started through those who had begun searching for answers to their questions, but stopped their journey too soon, unable to proceed further on their own. His revelation was required to extend their search for truth, to open their eyes to the whole truth of the God revealed in the Bible, and the Savior who died for their sins. As Jesus promised to His disciples, God will reveal whether what they believe originates from Him, from Satan, or from another human being who doesn't yet understand what is true and what is false:

"If any man will do His will, he shall know of the doctrine, whether it be of God, or whether I speak of myself" (John 7:17).

Then said Jesus to those Jews which believed on Him, "If you continue in my word, then are you my disciples indeed: and you shall know the truth, and the truth shall make you free" (John 8:31-32).

Through the good news of the Gospel of Christ, life or death, heaven or hell, and blessing or curse become choices in all our hands.

Now I understood that the author of all creation made His entry into the human world to satisfy our needs, to fill our hearts with His riches, to correct our misguided ways and to destroy evil within us and in the world. No longer was it my responsibility to turn the world from hell to heaven, but it was God's responsibility through those who have followed Him from the very beginning of human history. Jesus had already paved the way for the entire world to be saved, as long as they accept that way. What a relief!

I also delighted in learning about the God who revealed Himself first in the lives of the people in the Bible. I became acquainted with Noah, Abraham, Isaac, Jacob, and Joseph. I could feel their anguish through them, waiting for the Savior to come into the world. I learned the story of Moses, and about his suffering because of his work with the people of God. I loved each one, and decided the anguish I had experienced was nothing in comparison. I thanked God for their labor for me and for the world. They once walked the same earth I walk now. They felt the wind and the sun on their cheeks just as I do, and they must have thought and wondered and prayed about the same things which concern me. I ached with them and rejoiced with them, as God met all their needs, just as He was doing now for me.

No longer did I feel distant from the men and women of the Bible, just as I felt so near to my loved ones who lived and died before me in Japan. In Christ, the Lord of living and dead, we are people of "God with us," and we are not separated by death, by years, nor by cultures or colors of our skin. We are and always will be together in one purpose, to glorify God. Just as I felt so close to them, I also felt their presence with me. I am no longer alone in Christ. I wondered if missionaries who serve God in faraway places feel that same togetherness when they read the Bible or think of their families and Christian friends, and if they are comforted in their loneliness, too.

Another thought came to me as I read Matthew 17:20:

For verily I say unto you, if you have faith as a grain of mustard seed, you shall say unto this mountain, "Move from here to yonder place;" and it shall remove; and nothing shall be impossible unto you.

This must be the faith that moves God to act! If nothing is impossible with God, then couldn't He bring heaven down to earth, not just when Jesus was here, but now, as my childish mind had wanted so long ago? Couldn't he heal the daily news of war, hunger, killing, hurt, and destruction which make me, a mother, a woman and citizen of that earth very tired and sad?

Then one day my eyes read another of the unending truths from the Bible, and I nearly danced with joy:

*Our Father, which art in heaven, hallowed be thy
name. Thy Kingdom come, Thy will be done on earth
as it is in heaven...*(Matthew 6:9-10).

What a beautiful prayer! What a beautiful way to
express what I had so feebly desired. Like saving the world,
it wasn't just my idea to bring heaven to earth at all—it was
the Lord's Himself!

I thought my heart would burst with this new discovery.
My idea and my whole journey weren't childish dreams at
all, but the very plan of God! Even if this plan were not completed in my lifetime, I had faith to believe that one day the
words that revealed the heart of my Lord would be fulfilled,
triumphing in all of His creation. It was just as good as done
already.

But God must have been saving the best for last, for I
made the greatest discovery of all when I read the words of
Psalm 32:8:

*I will instruct thee and teach thee in the way which
thou shalt go: I will guide thee with mine eye.*

I couldn't take my eyes off those words! I was totally
overjoyed to know that the "eyes to see the truth" were real
after all. They were the eyes of my Lord Himself.

My heart could hardly hold the impact of this discovery,
that the Lord had been walking with me even when I didn't
know He was there. Those eyes, which had been behind my
eyes all that time, now faced me for the first time. How different from the time I had stood in the presence of the "eyes"
with my heavy, guilt-ridden conscience. I had left all my
upbringing behind, not knowing if I were doing right or
wrong, not knowing where my inner or outer journey would
take me, and feeling guilty for not knowing how to help a
world in turmoil. I was so troubled, feeling as if I were

responsible for everything that happened—even for the sins of Japan—because of my sin of omission.

I remembered thinking that the responsibility for my future belonged to the "eyes," because they had led me to the place where I saw my sinful condition in the first place. At one time, I thought I was destined to walk this journey alone, to be punished because I didn't know anything about my own life—let alone how to solve the problems of the world.

But now it was clear to me that God took, not some, but total responsibility for my life from its beginning to the end, which I still couldn't know, and throughout eternity. He covered my life with His own, protecting me, rescuing me from danger, and shielding me from Satan's accusation and the justice of God. No matter how deep my guilt, or how sinful I was, it didn't matter to Him, for He had died to cover the price of my sin and set me free from the power of darkness, Satan—*Enma*—himself. He has helped me grow in His knowledge totally free from worry and guilt. And I understood this was not only for myself, but for everyone who would accept his offer of salvation.

I recalled how I had challenged "the eyes to see the truth" for the first time at the railroad station in Japan, and the guidance came. Now, many years and discoveries later, He has unveiled Himself not just as eyes, but as light, as words for my mind to read and understand, as feet to walk before me, and the suffering Christ's presence deep within my heart, claiming me for His very own. Is there any greater love than this? None.

When I read about what Jesus said from His cross, praying for those who were crucifying him—"Father, forgive them for they know not what they do" (Luke 23:34), I immediately remembered what my grandmother had said to me in my childhood: "No matter what happens, you must forgive." Now I understood that my grandmother believed in forgiveness by faith, without ever knowing what Jesus said about forgiveness, or even what He did for each of us. But I lived to understand and meet the One who forgave us—even when we were the ones who caused Him to suffer and die. Because of what my grandmother told me, no matter what I did or what happened to me, I couldn't blame anyone else, for I did everything voluntarily anyway. Now I would no longer even have to blame myself.

I owe everything to Him, for without His death on the cross for me, I couldn't have made my journey from sin and ignorance to repentance, freedom, understanding, and peace. I would never have emerged from the dark night of my past to the morning sunrise of the "Light of the World."

Just as my father sent me out on a journey to seek the King of the whole world, I learned that God sent His only Son on a missionary journey to our world to seek the lost and bring them to salvation. Through my journey to seek the King of the whole world, I not only found that King, but I found out who I am—a child of that King, my Savior and my Lord. I also found the Holy Wisdom, Jesus Christ, who is able to turn the whole world around, and who is the only solution to all the world's problems.

My heart is filled with gratitude. Surely His ways and His thoughts are still beyond the understanding of a simple housewife and mother like me. But I am satisfied now, for I am no longer empty and hungry for things I don't understand. My life is full of meaning, purpose, and joy.

Blessed are all those who come to this truth, for by receiving the only begotten Son of God as their Savior and Lord, their life will be full of joy and meaning, too.

At that time Jesus, full of joy through the Holy Spirit, said, "I praise you, Father, Lord of heaven and earth, because you have hidden these things from the wise and learned, and revealed them to little children."...Then he turned to his disciples and said privately, "Blessed are the eyes that see what you see. For I tell you that many prophets and kings wanted to see what you see but did not see it, and to hear what you hear but did not hear it" (Luke 10:21,23; NIV).

Epilogue
RESPONSE

O give thanks unto the Lord, for he is good: for his mercy endureth forever. Let the redeemed of the Lord say so, whom he hath redeemed from the hand of the enemy; and gathered them out of the lands, from the East, and from the West, from the North, and from the South. They wandered in the wilderness in a solitary way; they found no city to dwell in. Hungry and thirsty, their soul fainted in them. Then they cried unto the Lord in their trouble, and he delivered them out of their distresses. And he led them forth by the right way, that they might go to a city of habitation. Oh, that men would praise the Lord for his goodness, and for his wonderful works to the children of men! For he satisfieth the longing soul, and filleth the hungry soul with goodness (Psalms 107:1-9).

What beautiful words to describe God's love for all His creatures, and what has happened in my own life. Without God, I have discovered, there is no value to life at all, but finding Him who sought me out is the greatest joy I have ever experienced.

As I observe the world, no matter who we are or where we come from, everyone longs for good things, yet there is so much that is not good in the world—even among religious organizations. Ungodly things like greed, envy, pride, and hatred create dark shadows between groups of people just as the earth blocks the light of the sun and creates the night. Like an eclipse that darkens the earth at midday, our sins prevent God's light and truth from shining through.

Just as I was led to seek this God of all creation, throughout history entire religions have been formed as people struggled to add happiness and meaning to their lives. But not everyone continued searching long enough to reach the Creator of life. Their ideas of the way, the truth, and the meaning of life differed widely according to the quality of their hearts, which determined the depth and width of their search. Depending on the amount of truth they received, some groups continued to shine dimly, while others gave out more light in their effort to attract larger groups of people. Some religions are also discovering new insights as they become enlightened in the knowledge of the truth. Whether bright or dim, however, the purpose was the same: to separate their people from the way of evil, and sustain them through the long journey of their lives.

No wonder there have been so many religions under so many spiritual leaders throughout human history! Throngs have searched for that light with only their own understanding (Proverbs 3:5), without knowledge of their Creator who wanted to teach, guide, and reveal the blessed way of life through His book, *The Holy Bible*. Religions differ from each other like the moon in its varying shapes and brightness, but, in the partial light of the night, they never can enjoy the abundant life of the daytime sun, a life of fellowship with the Creator, God Almighty: His Fatherhood, and His presence.

At the beginning of my journey, I knew there was something very wrong with the world, and I thought wisdom was necessary to solve its problems. I was not sure, however, where I would find this wisdom. Now, knowing that this wisdom is Jesus Christ, I can see how the blessings and presence of the Creator have been behind those smaller lights all along to care for and sustain the lost world of the night. He has proven to me His merciful, unlimited love for those whose consciences are alive through faith to an invisible God by gathering them under religious leaders throughout the darkened world.

Yet religions without the knowledge of the true, living God are incomplete, and they are kept forever under the reflection of the true light. It is our unbelief in the living God that allows the darkness to keep us in its power like stars in the dark summer night. Though these countless stars attract us with their mystical beauty from the deep, dark beyond, they can't extinguish the darkness even with the help of the full moon.

So, it is time to wake up, accept that truth, and end the nightmare of the night in our world by inviting the "light of the world" (John 9:5) into our lives. For it is the matter of our will whether we let ungodly things like crime and hatred multiply in the darkness or expose them in the true light for our cleansing and healing. Where there is no light, there is no vision either (Proverbs 29:18).

It is time to examine ourselves in the bright, morning sun, the Son of God, Jesus Christ who is that true light "which lighteth every man that cometh into the world" (John 1:9). Christ is that light for me, and more. He guides me, feeds me, and provides all that I need. He satisfies me with Himself even as a skillful heavenly surgeon.

My night is definitely over, for I have found God, the origin and source of faith. Just as a traveler must get out of his vehicle when he arrives at his destination, I had to leave Buddhism behind when I reached my destination—the person of Jesus Christ, the Truth whom God sent. To me, Christianity is a way of life revealed by God the Creator to man, or comes from heaven to earth; while Buddhism involves man seeking and reaching up to God, coming from earth to heaven. The Father's way is much more direct, with God initiating a fulfilling relationship between the believer and Himself.

God can use anything to accomplish His plan of salvation. God's loving searchlight toward me began with the teachings of Buddha, which were transmitted through people who believed them and taught them to me, and then burst into blazing floodlights when I learned it was God's love that brought me home to Himself at the end of my journey through the night.

But when I thought my journey was over, I realized it was just beginning. Yes, my journey centered around self was over, but my journey to do the will of the King of the universe was about to begin. It's a source of great joy for me to know that the "eyes" which guided me during the first phase of my journey in the wilderness are continuing to direct my path.

I remember how delighted I was to work with the farmers, learning to do their work in my childhood. Now, with childlike excitement, I am even more delighted to learn and do God's work, in His world and in His way.

In the late 1970's, after the Army had sent Tom to Augusta, Georgia, for his final military assignment, and I had spent several years growing as a Christian, I had a dream which I won't forget for the rest of my life.

The white, cottony cloud floated softly through the blue sky before my eyes. I watched as a man's fingertips appeared from the midst of it. Slowly a hand and then an arm emerged, appearing to direct the hand downward. Both the hand and arm were sheathed in well-toned muscles, streaked with pulsating veins, and glowing with a light brighter than sunlight. The skin appeared to be breathing as the downy hair covering the arm reflected that light. I knew instantly it was the right arm of the Lord.

As my eyes followed the downward movement of the hand, I saw what looked like a massive pile of junk coming into view. But as the pile and the hand drew closer together, I saw that the pile was actually the surface of the earth covered with toppled buildings, demolished cars, broken television sets, and other dilapidated, useless things. The whole earth, all civilization it seemed, lay in ruins, as if consumed by a mammoth earthquake. It was very sad to look at such a terrible sight.

But then, as I kept watching, I saw the hand of the Lord reach deeply into the pile and begin searching for something with His fingertips. He chose several items and pulled them out of the pile in His closed palm. My sadness lifted and I became excited, wondering what He had chosen so carefully from the bottom of all that debris.

Just then I woke up, realized I had been dreaming, and knew I would never know what the Lord had brought out of the ruined earth.

Morning was still hours away, but I couldn't go back to sleep. I rose, wandered through the house, and tried to figure out what the dream meant. I asked the Lord what it meant. Was there some message in it for me? Knowing of the Lord's great love for the earth—His own creation—I could understand His arm stretching out toward it, even though it lay in ruins. I also thought, maybe this is what the earth looks like to Him anyway. Could it be that what He had pulled from the ruins were His people, those who believed in Him, and He was rescuing them from all that devastation? The arm could mean the Gospel of Christ, but....

A few days later I asked my pastor what he thought my dream meant. He said it could be just a blessing from the Lord, but that he didn't see any particular message to it. Though I didn't worry about the dream anymore, it was never far from my mind. Some years later I related the dream to a dear Christian sister. The dream was positively from the Lord, she said, but she had no words to explain its meaning. "But," she continued, "if there is a meaning, the Lord will reveal it to you."

One Sunday morning more than fifteen years later while worshiping God in a small church, the meaning of the dream suddenly became clear to me:

The ruined civilization is a spiritual view of the corrupt world condemned by God. I had been right about what He plucked from the ruins; it was His people. Those He "hand-picked" are His chosen ones whom He empowers and unites to carry out His purpose for those who are immature in His Word and reach out to those who are still living in the night with His Gospel (see John 17; Romans 15:1-13). The right arm of the Lord reveals His responsibility to deliver those who trust Him, including nations that acknowledge God in Christ, from the bondage under Satan's power, and establish a new earth under the reign of Christ. The light glowing from the arm is to assure them of His presence while His work is being done on earth. However, I don't know when this will take place.

This dream reminded me again of another one I had many years before, when I felt myself falling in the darkness for so long with great fear, but was awakened by lightning in the dream before any harm could come to me. Before I woke, however, the lightning revealed I was near the entrance of a tunnel where I could look through and see the dawning sky above wet, swaying trees in a clean, open field. As I pondered that dream at the time, I thought I couldn't have been falling, but must have been pulled out of the darkness toward the dawn and into the peaceful aftermath of the storm. And I remember how glad those thoughts made me feel, and how they wiped the fear away from me.

Now, in the aftermath of my latter dream, I believe it was the arm of the Lord in the former dream, too, rescuing

142

me from a dark world and bringing me to the place of light, peace, and knowledge of Himself. As I would learn later, it is God who comes to claim all those who believe in Him and follow His words. He is like the Shepherd in John 10:16, calling those "other sheep" who will "hear my voice, and follow me...."

Because of my hunger to know the truth, God pulled me out of my dark world into the light of His world and taught me about Himself. Most importantly, He made Himself known to me, not just so I would believe in Him, but so I would also join Him to do His will with trust built by experience with Him. It is my duty now, as well as my desire, to follow that call so His will can be done on earth.

Long ago as I began my journey, I wished I could help others in their struggles of life, too, and that I could find the wisdom to bring heaven down to earth. I can't do that myself, in my own strength, but I have found the One who can and desires to do so. So I wait for His exact instructions to be revealed by His Spirit and through His Word, so that He can use me for His purpose.

Though anguish and pain always accompanied my journey as a fool frog in the world, today I know the suffering I endured was carrying the weight of my ignorance about the true knowledge of the living God, the Creator of all. I recall fondly the memory of the young barley I stamped down upon with the farmer's wife in my childhood. Like those plants, surely the pain and anguish didn't destroy me, but they instead strengthened me: I experienced a glimpse of the suffering Christ went through for the world and for me.

When I became a mother I remember feeling guilty because I wasn't able to teach my own children about the real God or the true way of life. Furthermore, I didn't know how to protect them from the forces in the world that counter our efforts to teach our children Christian principles for their daily lives. There were no assurances that they would be fine if we died before they matured. But these thoughts made me aware of the needs of others who might be suffering from a similar dilemma. Like my grandfather before me, I knew that to help my own children, I must desire the well-being of other parents' children, too. We all have common needs, but how important is the responsibility of parents, especially a mother, to build the character of her child at an early stage, and let the child know about the blessedness of the love of God in His children.

As the Japanese proverb, "If you love your child, send him on a journey," declares, all children learn best by experience. They learn how to judge bad behavior from good, and how to gain love, peace, and happiness, not by avoiding the pain and toil of life, but by enduring it and learning to give the same love to others that they hope to obtain for themselves. I have learned that not everyone reaches this conclusion, but those who use their journey for their own selfish gain seldom reap the happiness they expected to find.

I realize parents must prepare their children for their journey, too, for the journey itself is a testing tool to determine the quality of the relationship between the parent, the child, and other people. It seems that life on earth is a journey from which no one can escape, and which will surely test the quality of one's heart.

Even as I look ahead, I continue to ponder how the journey of a Buddhist's daughter in search of the King of the whole world became the journey of a daughter of the heavenly Father in Christ. Following my earthly father's wishes when I was a small child progressed to seeking my heavenly Father's will now that I am grown. Without realizing it at the time, I was after the most important knowledge in the world when I set out to find that imaginary king in my father's story about those two frogs!

But my journey was far from an imaginary one, and the truth which God is teaching me is far from a minor, unimportant story. I'm learning that life without the true and living God is a life of sin, rebellion, and death, all of which produce the short supply of love, joy, peace, and understanding we find in our family life and society today.

No wonder the deeper my interest in the human struggle became, the more my anguish and suffering increased. The more I searched, the more I learned about my own sin, too. The eyes to see the truth discerned my own pride, laziness, hidden ambition, dishonest excuses, and other sins which my heart produced as prolifically as our backyard produced weeds.

And my own heart was a mirror to the world! With the Lord's guidance, I learned that when these baby evil spirits mature and take root in the flesh, they become the beasts of the fields, the asphalt jungles in our cities, and the wickedness so apparent throughout our society. Human beings without the indwelling Spirit of God have no control over their own desires, but are controlled by them instead. Rather than exhibiting the fruits of the Holy Spirit (Galatians 5:22-23) as God intended, their lives reveal the far less loving, joyful, and peaceful traits which Satan inflicts on those who are controlled by him.

Once, during my early growth as a Christian, I saw my pride as a fast-growing mushroom enticing me to lean against it and be comforted by the stronghold of self-satisfaction, and my conscience became inflamed. Pride is a deadly, spiritual cancer, I've learned, capable of replacing the very presence of God in our lives, and pulling us down below the level of life He created us to live.

I understood why the Lord, and His "eyes to see the truth," had led me to inspect myself inwardly (Proverbs 20:27), just as I know now that all women, and men, too, have been affected by the venom of the "Serpent" from the very beginning of human history. As the Apostle John writes: "(They) still live to satisfy the lust of the flesh, and the lust of the eyes, and the pride of life which is not of the Father, but is of the world" (1 John 2:16).

How true it is! Selfish ambition often overshadows the responsibilities of fathers and mothers, and, sadly, children are starving for the spiritual nourishment which they need to receive from their parents just as much as they need physical food.

At times I, too, was doing all that noble searching just to satisfy myself and my own pride, and "the eyes to know the truth" had to point out even that to me. Now I can see that it is pride in all of us that builds walls within families and between societies, churches, and the tribes and nations of the world. Pride is Satan's altar, his method of putting the whole world under his power, forcing one person or nation against another instead of guiding them to forgive each other.

But by trusting God's power instead of my own, I could forget about myself and do away with the pride that was once strong in my life. I thank the Lord for His Word which provides me with this understanding. Reading Jeremiah 17:9 was a great comfort to me:

> *The heart is deceitful above all things....(but) I the Lord search the heart...and give to every man according to his ways, and according to the fruit of his doings.*

All my deficiencies, everything I've ever done, are understood and forgiven by my loving God as I confess my sins to Him.

When I came to America, I was still a citizen of Japan, the loser in the great war between those two nations. But I have learned that the winner of any war is still a loser. No one wins in a war but Satan. Therefore, it is better to choose the way of life of Christ, the true victor, instead of Satan's way of death, in order to avoid the endless turmoil of war after war in this world, and the fight for ethnic pride, political power, or self-gratification.

Finally I learned that Jesus came into my life in order to replace my sinful, earthly self (Ephesians 4:22-24), and to help me keep my eyes on Him and my hands doing His will. This way I remain His possession. "And the world passeth away, and the lust thereof: but he that doeth the will of God abideth forever" (1 John 2:17). Jesus has pointed out to me that, if I do what is right in my own understanding or without death to self, I might end up building the "kingdom of myself" in His name, or choosing to follow the spirit of man rather than the Holy Spirit of God. Though it required major spiritual surgery on my heart, the heavenly physician, Jesus, has fulfilled all my desires, answered all my questions, and taught me to live in His righteousness by faith through His Word.

The Lord exhibited His divine ability to meet my needs and made my impossible journey possible when there were no visible footsteps for me to follow. He created a path for me where there was no path, for He Himself was the way. So I rejoice in Him, and bless His Name for His goodness. When I look at the world situation, however, sadness overwhelms me. How I wish all the people of the earth could experience the joy of knowing the love of Jesus, and could live in peace with one another!

Helplessly, I can only remember again the stranger's voice so long ago in Japan: "What will you do if you find the answers you are looking for?" I answered then that I would give them to the man to whom people will listen, for I knew no one would listen to an uneducated woman like me. But now I know that Man—Jesus Christ, the Son of God, the One who gave all these answers to me. He is the only One to whom people should listen, for He is both the solution to all our needs and the greatest Communicator of that solution to the world.

I know now that Jesus won the victory in my life, both against Satan and the darkness of my ignorance about God, long before I knew the battle was going on. He was with me in the wilderness called "the world" for my entire life, in good times and bad, making Himself known to me, a Buddhist who willingly became a Christian in order to know the other, "sunny" side of the world under God.

In the light of the life and teaching of Christ, my journey as a Christian caused me to re-examine the heart of Buddha's teaching, to love, to be kind, and to be merciful to all living things. When Christ was introduced to me as my Savior and Lord, I didn't yet know much about Him, but I sensed that it was the will of God for me to become a Christian by faith. For without becoming one, there was no way of knowing who Christ was. To reject Christ would have been a disgrace to Buddhism, which taught us to love and be kind to even a stranger.

Following this new Christ was a very painful decision for me, but His patience was far greater than my stubbornness. He guided my slow steps forward by the positive understanding that, although Christianity and Buddhism are so different, both existed for the similar purpose of bringing peace and joy on earth. But Jesus makes all the difference as to the type of joy and peace we should have. By following His example, we Christians learn to love our enemies, bringing us lasting peace and joy in Him.

He proved to me that He is who He is without any room for argument. This is what sets apart Christianity from Buddhism or any other religion. All *earthly* religions are missing this knowledge of true creator God, and without this knowledge, no religion can reach its goal. Only in Christ, who took our sins away, we can have true peace and maturity.

Buddhism taught me to love and be merciful to all living things, even all creation. That teaching prepared me to have a sensitive heart when a stranger is introduced to us.

Certainly Christ was a stranger to me at first, and meeting Him in the reality of day-to-day life was even more difficult for me: Jesus, the Creator in human flesh, wanted me to know Him! How glad I am that, with trembling heart, without knowing if I were doing right or wrong, I took those painful early steps. I felt I had to follow my instincts. When I did, I found the eternal treasure!

But why was it that important to Him to help me in my enormous need? When I asked myself that question, I remembered again the dream of "the arm of the Lord," and immediately I knew the work I was called to do. Although I am unworthy, I understood that Jesus desired my cooperation to enlarge my own spiritual "sunrise," so that His sunrise— the power of His resurrection—could reach Japanese, Buddhists, and others in the world as well.

People all over the earth have been walking in the realm of the night, too, though some have journeyed on, led by their faith in God and guided by His messengers, the prophets. It became clear to me that the greater light of truth, "the Light of the world," must rise in the east. Jesus Christ, the Savior of the world, must be known in Japan for it to truly be called the "land of the rising sun."

Jesus Christ will usher in a spiritual sunrise, breaking the dawn of a new day on earth! God, who created day and night, had been waiting for the right time for morning to arrive on this dark world. But according to the law of creation, the morning will not come unless the sun rises in the east, and night yields to day. In the same manner as the physical sunrise, Christ, the Enlightening One, desires to illuminate the land by His Gospel. It will be just as it is written in 1 Corinthians 15:54:

When the perishable has been clothed with the imperishable, and the mortal with immortality, then the saying that is written will come true: "Death has been swallowed up in victory."

How magnificent the spiritual sunrise will be, that moment when the night and day become one according to God's plan. His light will shine forth evenly on earth, uniting the day (people with knowledge of God in Christ) and the night (people without the knowledge of God in Christ), bringing the love and truth of His Gospel to all.

Spiritually speaking, only Jesus can create the dawn of enlightenment. He called Himself "the morning star" in Revelation 22:16:

> *I Jesus sent mine angel to testify unto you these things in the churches. I am the root and the offspring of David, and the bright and morning star.*

It will be the beginning of a new era, when the whole earth acknowledges His truth, and when "the peace that passes all understanding" (Philippians 4:7) passes between Jew and Gentile, husband and wife, father and mother, children and parents, the visible and invisible, the spiritual and physical, uniting them all according to the original purpose of His creation: to glorify His mighty name. As it is written, "...without Him was not anything made that was made" (John 1:3), it is about time for this truth to be recognized, and His creation to be reconciled according to the purpose of its Maker. Then, finally, heaven and earth will be one.

As He said, "I am the beginning and the end" (see Revelation 1:8), this new spiritual morning must be the beginning of a new day, an end to the old things of the past on earth. His creation record in Genesis 1:31 describes one day in the following terms:

> *God saw all that He had made, and it was very good. And there was evening and there was morning—the sixth day* (NIV).

God's creation was "very good." Adam and Eve (and mankind ever since) sinned. His cross is the place of a new beginning, a new day, a spiritual morning, to end the thing of old. His cross restores the goodness of man, God's creation.

Once, on a high mountain slope in Japan, I experienced a sunrise so beautiful—the contrasting light and darkness seemed to display the powerful unveiling light of the sun upon the earth. As the rising sun lifted the darkness from the chilly air, the high and low mountain peaks, the perfect balance between depth and plain, and the limitless space beyond the horizon all blended with the song of waking birds and the panoramic view of a towering, misty rainbow in the valley below. All the elements of creation, all equal, melted into one holy splendor, glorifying not the parts but the One who had created them all. The limitless space suffused with warm light seemed to hug all visible creation high and low, large or small in its arms, giving value to all life as the darkness was peeled away by the light. And because of the living touch of God, I was more than a spectator of this unforgettable view. I was a part of that creation, too, which bespoke the artistry of its Creator.

Now I know why my father bought me those books about the sun, the moon, and the stars. Though he left the choice in my hand when he asked me which frog was the wise one in his story, I believe he knew I would continue searching until I found the King of the whole world after he opened up for me a world, a universe, much wider than the small village or even the country where I lived, which was controlled by the emperor in those days.

Now I know I was my father's gift to that King God, in whom my father believed by faith. In the midst of an uncertain world, he left my care in the hand of God by pointing me toward Him, hoping I would seek and find Him as he passed away from my life. I also know for certain that, as an educator, he knew I would obtain new, true knowledge if I ever reached Him, and return to help those who live under false gods, controlled by incomplete, earthly religions and superstitions because they have no knowledge of the true, living God.

Many people worship human spirits or some human hero as their god. The Bible tells us the origin of this practice in Genesis 3:4-5:

And the serpent said unto the woman, Ye shall not surely die: for God doth know that in the day ye eat thereof, then your eyes shall be opened, and ye shall be as gods, knowing good and evil.

So, it was Satan in the background of human lives, who deceived men and women to become as gods (a sin of high treason against the true God) so he could take God's place and separate people from Him. Now I see Shintoism (the ways of gods) was developed under Satan's deceptive lie, as I understand by reading 2 Corinthians 11:14-15:

Satan himself is transformed into an angel of light. Therefore it is no great thing if his ministers also be transformed as the ministers of righteousness; whose end shall be according to their works.

The Bible also tells the story of how Satan tempted the Son of God concerning the kingdoms of the world:

Again, the devil taketh him up into an exceeding high mountain, and sheweth him all the kingdoms of the world, and the glory of them, and saith unto Him, "All these things will I give thee, if thou wilt fall down and worship me." Then saith Jesus unto him, "Get thee hence, Satan: for it is written, 'Thou shalt worship the Lord thy God, and him only shalt thou serve.'" Then the devil leaveth him, and, behold, angels came and ministered unto Him (Matthew 4:8-10).

Satan has been playing this same game with leaders of the world in various fields and governments, capitalizing on human weakness—pride, greed, ambition and desire—by offering them what they hope to possess through his system of "I'm right, you are wrong," and "I'm better than you," to draw them into the world of conflict, violence, and competition.

It is painful to know and write about how Satan cleverly closed what could be interpreted "the east gate" of the earth, Japan, with the false spiritual sun (*Amaterasu-Omikami*), focusing attention on a creation instead of the Creator, to keep the world in his shadow. But I conclude it is even more painful to live continuously under Satan's dark domain when the Great Light reveals the truth about our condition, along with His solution.

The love of God can overcome the evil caused by ignorance, sin, and the influence of Satan over people. The power of Christ's cross, blood, name, and word have yet to be experienced in fullness by most people on the earth. His Gospel demands that people choose between truth and falsehood, light and darkness, eternal life and eternal death, Himself and Satan. When Christ's power is released, people will choose, and the harvest will be reaped.

Although it is unbelievable to me that my journey has come to this point, I do believe I was born into my particular set of circumstances to live, to search, to understand, and to write this testimony. I believe it is God who created this testimony to make Himself known to them who, through Satan's deception, have been kept under the bondage of sin for so long. This is the reason Jesus was sent to the world: God took the responsibility upon Himself to save a lost world.

The Spirit of the Lord is upon me, because he hath anointed me to preach the gospel to the poor, he hath sent me to heal the broken hearted, to preach deliverance to the captives, and recovering of sight to the blind, to set at liberty them that are bruised, to preach the acceptable year of the Lord (Luke 4:18-19).

What a wonderful act of love He manifested in His life toward fallen mankind!

I believe the Holy Spirit of God used Buddhism, too, to sustain me and others in my part of the world through our time of darkness and suffering until Christ, the morning sun, came to us. For if anyone's faith is based on a truth such as love for all mankind, which is a reflection of the love of God, that goodwill shall produce spiritual fruit in due season, for those seeking to do the Father's will. It is my prayer that everyone may see Him as He is, the true "light of men":

In him was life, and that life was the light of men. The light shines in the darkness and the darkness has not overcome it (John 1:4-5).

I can understand now how difficult it was for my father, a Buddhist, to follow the government of his day under Shintoism, and I am glad he encouraged me to seek the "Lord of creation" and the "King of the whole world." I realize now that I loved Buddha in my childhood because my family said he loved everybody, not only the Japanese. All that made sense to me then, and prepared the way for me to know God, "who so loved the world that He gave His only begotten Son..." (John 3:16). Praise God who knows our needs and caught me, taught me, and purified me.

I remember an incident in my childhood which indicated that I not only had to overcome my own failures and shortcomings, but those of Japan—the work of the serpent on earth.

It was a clear autumn day after the harvest. I was playing in the wide, open field near my grandparents' house. My grandfather called me to come to him. He was broiling something on a large grill in the middle of the field. My grandmother sat on a stool nearby. The blue smoke rose high into the sky. No one else was around—except God as I know now. My grandfather lifted up a broiled *mamushi* (poisonous snake) with long iron chopsticks. He broke off a piece from its tail and gave it to me to eat. My grandmother smiled at me as I put it in my mouth. I was about two years old.

I remembered this incident about a year ago, at the age of sixty-one, and thought that in the light of what I have learned from Scripture, my life was given to God by my grandparents at an early age to help destroy the work of Satan. I had to recognize the sin of the woman in the Garden of Eden, as well as my own sins, in order to be forgiven. Then my Savior, Jesus Christ, could remove the work of Satan from my life, replace it with Himself, and prepare me to do His will on earth (see John 16:7-11).

Sometime later I learned that the cooperation of the woman, and then the man in the garden, with the "serpent" (a universal word describing Satan, the enemy of God) allowed the entrance of Satan's will into the human race. Mankind traces its fall to the sin of Adam and Eve. Therefore, women had to be part of the spiritual exodus out of Satan's kingdom into the kingdom of God in Christ, the Messiah. I didn't fully understand this concept at the time. Then I had another dream which convinced me of its truth:

In my dream, I remember vividly a sharp pain on my right side below the rib cage. Groaning with pain, I saw what looked like the top of a cane trying to push through my side from within. Then I woke up, thankful to be relieved of the pain!

Immediately I remembered how God provided a helpmate for Adam by taking one of his ribs and creating the first woman, and I remembered one of Christ's disciples was taken out of the group, comparing the two instances. God provided woman as helpmate for man, and He provided for the apostles when one of their number left the fold. In both cases, He made man complete. So it was also His responsibility to complete

155

His work in the woman as her Creator and Savior (He created and saved her, just as He did the man), so that He can work through woman, redeeming her responsibility for the condition of the world, fully renewing His first creation.

So God created man in his own image, in the image of God he created him; male and female he created them (Genesis 1:27).

Both men and women are equally human, capable of sinning, and can be redeemed by Christ to respond to God's grace. Therefore, just as her weakness contributed to the fall of man in the Garden of Eden, the woman's cooperation is equally necessary to make man's redemption complete. Just as He created them, He would redeem them—male and female.

But our human inclination to sin passed from Adam and Eve to Cain. Because God was pleased by Abel's offering, and displeased by Cain's, Cain killed his brother out of jealousy. Therefore, God sent Cain away from His presence—just like Adam and Eve:

God said to Cain, if you had done the right thing, you would be smiling, but because you have done evil, sin is crouching at your door. It wants to rule you, but you must overcome it (Genesis 4:7, GNB).

But why does the power of sin remain a constant threat to rule over man? It is always man's choice whether or not to eat of "the tree of the knowledge of good and evil" (Genesis 2:17). This tree represents life in union with the serpent, Satan, which produces "good and evil," while "the tree of life," which represents life in union with God, produces "good" only.

But when our first parents ate the fruit of the forbidden tree, and committed spiritual adultery with Satan, the whole human race came under the bondage of Satan's "sin-nature," and became part of his rebellion against God. What a tragedy!

Deprived of God's grace, we became incapable of choosing God's way of life (partaking of "the tree of life"). But thanks be to God for his unspeakable gift from heaven, Jesus Christ, who provided the way back to God, to enjoy our lives united with Him (see John 3:16, 14:6; Matthew 6:9-13; and 2 Cor. 9:15). At the same time that Jesus feeds us from "the tree of life," He teaches us to reorient our thinking, so that we refrain from eating of the "tree of the knowledge of good and evil," through the power of His Spirit.

I was born in the East, in Japan—*Nihon*, "the place of the rising sun"—where the physical sun rose every morning with unmistakable accuracy, but the spiritual sun, which was supposed to enlighten the hearts and minds of all mankind on earth with the true knowledge of the living God, our Creator, never shined for me until Jesus came into my life. As a spiritual being, I needed the spiritual light of the Son just as much, or more than, my physical being needed physical light for my life on earth.

So, just as my name *Chiga*—which means "a thousand or eternal blessings or celebration"—didn't fit me before I was "born again" by the Spirit of God, the name *Nihon*, "the place of the rising sun," won't fit Japan until her people recognize the true Creator. The god of Japan, the sun goddess, could not bring forth light to the whole world, only darkness. Without recognizing the God who created the earth, its sun, moon, and stars, *Nihon's* spiritual dimension is not yet born. Only the Creator of earth could be the God of earth, and true Light of the world.

The country called, "one nation under God," America, needs to learn the same lesson. America has become one nation under many gods, and therefore does not now fit what it claims to be.

As a matter of fact, the whole world doesn't make sense to me, no matter which way I look at it. Spiritually speaking, the earth is still without form, and void; and darkness is upon the face of the deep (Genesis 1:2). May the Spirit of God move upon the face of the nations to recreate and bless them, and may the world experience a new beginning through the Gospel of Jesus Christ.

May all the nations be born again to give honor and glory to their Creator, and to "the Lamb of God who takes away the sins of the world" (John 1:29). He died on the cross and rose to reign over His united world. True peace on earth depends on the unity of all peoples and nations under the one, true God.

His creation earth was lost to Satan by Adam and Eve. It was Jesus who bought it back with His priceless Blood almost 2,000 years ago. Therefore, He is the rightful owner of the earth, and it is His right to adjust and align (spiritually purify) this corrupt, visible world into the yet to be known kingdom of God on earth.

As a witness of what Jesus Christ has done in my life, I am responding now to His call to "let the redeemed of the Lord say so!" (Psalm 107:2) This book is written for the same reason the Lord said to the Apostle Paul a long time ago:

I now send thee, to open their eyes and turn them from darkness to light, and from the power of Satan unto God, that they may receive forgiveness of sins, and an inheritance among them which are sanctified by faith in me (Acts 26:17-18).

Epilogue
HIS CROSS

Over the years since I became a Christian, I have had a difficult time learning about my new faith in churches of different cities and towns where I have lived. I have tried to understand why I found it so difficult to live what I came to believe in Christ. The divisions in Christianity concerned me greatly. Over and over I was drawn to search for ways to help the Church be a united Body. I knew this was not the will of God for His Church (division wounds God's heart, and is also Satan's method of conquest—"divide and conquer"). We may be at different stages in our spiritual growth, but I felt we could be one-minded in speaking His truth, carrying out His commandments, and glorifying His Name on earth in response to His love for us.

I believe, although it was allowed by the grace of God, the creation of divisions by both denominational and non-denominational churches was Satan's work through our human weakness (eating from "the tree of the knowledge of good and evil"). I believe also, according to His promise in Matthew 28:20, Jesus has been with us covering our sins with His blood whenever divisions were created, and He continued to use them for His benefit to spread His Gospel while we were still blind and immature.

Yet sin is sin. The darkness crept into His Body to separate us from each other. Generally speaking, the Body of Christ is spiritually weakened and exists feebly today (compared to what it could be) against the power of darkness as a whole, because of the divisions caused by lack of love and faith, and the true knowledge of God, self, and Satan according to the teaching of the Scriptures. For we cannot know God, self, or Satan without obeying God's commandments (see Hebrews 4:10-13; John 8:31-32; and Hosea 4:6).

Knowing the end from the beginning (Isaiah 46:10), Jesus who came to destroy the work of Satan in the world (1 John 3:8), must have prayed the prayer of John 17:21 two thousand years ago to keep His Body united in Him, in order to resist Satan for such a time as ours today:

That they may be one, Father, just as you are in me and I am in you. May they also be in us so that the world may believe you have sent me (NIV).

His prayer was answered by God, the Father, in the lives of His original disciples, including Judas who betrayed Him. Judas fell away because his God was his "self." I understood this as fulfillment of the Scripture Genesis 3:15. While Satan bruised His heel by taking one of His disciples (His Body), Christ bruised Satan's head upon His cross, and removed the power of Satan from ruling over the world through sin, and opened the way of salvation for mankind. The space created by Judas could be considered the door to welcome Gentile believers into the household of Christ, called His Church.

However, the Lord's prayer for us to be one in Him has not yet been fulfilled by today's Christianity. When I question this matter, the answer I get from many ministers is: "Don't worry about it, when Jesus returns, He will make us one."

Then I wondered, if it is so, why did Jesus pray for us to be one instead of telling us that He will do so when He comes again? I remembered His very words from John 15:5:

I am the vine, ye are the branches: He that abideth in me, and I in him, the same bringeth forth much fruit: for without me ye can do nothing.

If we ignore His prayer for unity, and detach ourselves (branches) from Him (the vine), we seem to ignore God and push Him out of our lives. Isn't this an open rebellion against God?

In Matthew 28:20, Jesus told His apostles to teach people "to observe all things whatsoever I have commanded you." I believe, therefore, His commandment to love:

You shall love one another, as I have loved you. Greater love hath no man than this, that a man lay down his life for his friends (John 15:12-13).

This commandment to love and the prayer for unity should be honored in obedience so that "the pearl of great price" (Christ) may be displayed in public to magnify His name. I believe it was very important to God, for Jesus not only commanded, but prayed for, our oneness in Him. Our disobedience to His teachings means to throw our pearls away before His enemies, so they can use them to weaken us, His body.

Give not that which is holy unto the dogs, neither cast ye your pearls before swine, lest they trample them under their feet, and turn again and rend you (Matthew 7:6).

If God, who is greater than division, desired to be known, and sent His only begotten Son for that purpose, it will be His innermost desire to manifest Himself in the lives of believers first, in order to reach the whole world. His command to "love one another as I have loved you," or His desire for us to be "in one accord" for the glory of God, can't be only for a family or a local church, or even within a group of churches. His new commandment and prayer were for the entire Christian community under His name, to keep His

161

Body as one in Him by His Spirit. "...And there shall be one fold and one shepherd" (John 10:16).

Quite easily earthly traditions can exalt themselves above God, and limit the work of the Lord with man-made doctrines, which block the way of the Lord. Unsound doctrine may be attractive and appear to be the truth in our human understanding, but it is deadly at the core. We find this in 2 Timothy 4:3-4:

For the time will come when men will not put up with sound doctrine. Instead, to suit their own desires, they will gather around them a great number of teachers to say what their itching ears want to hear. They will turn their ears away from the truth and turn aside to myths (NIV).

Error is like a cancerous tumor in a human body: it slowly but surely destroys the intended work of God. First Satan subtly takes away the wisdom of God from His people, replacing it with man-made doctrines which remove the fear of the Lord. Thus, when he cuts off the source of wisdom from above in believers, he destroys their ability to depart from evil (see Job 28:28). Man-made doctrines lead us to become man-centered Christians who reject the presence of God before we even realize it.

I believe the Scriptures reveal the faithfulness and love of our Lord and Savior (see John 10:28; Romans 8:35-39; Ephesians 1:12-14, 4:30; and Philippians 1:6), but I also take His warnings seriously, since He gave them to us, also out of love. Christ warned:

But whoso shall offend one of these little ones which believe in me, it were better for him that a millstone were hanged about his neck, and that he were drowned in the depth of the sea (Matthew 18:6).

Satan distorts the truth and tries to make believers think that God doesn't mean what He says in order to supplant God's place in believers' lives ("You surely will not die" Genesis 3:4). Satan can use the words, "Once you are saved, you are always saved," to destroy young faith or seduce believers to do wrong by causing some to willfully fall away from the faith, when we ignore His warning (Hebrews 6:4-8,10,22-31).

I believe that man-made truths, which replace the Word of God, are introduced to believers through deception by the territorial spirits assigned by the god of this world. Each "religious" spirit is a familiar spirit whose job is to guard and protect man-made doctrines, binding and blinding believers with the authority and power given by the enemy of God. These spirits deceive men through pride and self-righteousness enticing them to become like gods who know "good and evil," "right and wrong" (Genesis 3:5). In this way they replace the Lordship of Christ with false doctrines and the godhead of self, and build their stronghold *within* Christianity (see Ephesians 6:12).

Instead of placing Christ's commandments under our own authority, we need to place ourselves *under His commands* to obey and honor Him. Jesus who came, lived, died, and rose again (1 Corinthians 15:1-5), said to believers: "Pick up your own cross and follow me" (Matthew 16:24).

Now I can understand what Jesus taught in the parables of the "Sower and the Seed" (Matthew 13:24-30). Surely His enemy sowed his seed among the children of God in an underhanded, crafty manner. Ever since the fall of Adam, children of "good and evil" were born from the same parents, works of "good and evil" stemmed from the same person, and both "praise and curse" proceeded from the same mouth.

Saddest of all are the divisions within the Church. Even though I attend church regularly, it is very difficult for me to join a particular church, especially after I have seen the divided condition of today's Christianity. I long to see Christ's Body function in a unified way.

> *How good and pleasant it is when brothers live together in unity!* (Psalm 133:1, NIV)

How tragic it is to see that many churches are blinded by not believing in the supernatural gifts of the Holy Spirit (see 1 Corinthians 12:1–11). When we reject His gifts, His work in and through us becomes limited, if not thwarted. This unbelief also causes His Body to be divided and, therefore, much less effective.

Satan can't take the supernatural gifts of the Holy Spirit away from Him. But through people's unbelief, Satan deprives many churches from receiving God's unique powers, causing them to refuse His ministries (the love of God in action) through His Church. Under the above conditions, in spite of our efforts, it seems impossible to reach unity in the faith and in the knowledge of the Son of God and become mature, attaining to the whole measure of the fullness of Christ.

> *....so that the Body of Christ may be built up until we all reach unity in the faith and in the knowledge of the Son of God and become mature, attaining to the whole measure of the fullness of Christ....speaking the truth in love, we will in all things grow up into Him who is the head, that is, Christ. From Him the whole Body, joined and held together by every supporting ligament, grows and builds itself up in love, as each part does its work* (Ephesians 4:12-13,15-16, NIV).

I believe it is so important for us to believe, keep His commandments, and become doers of His words. What a glorious day it will be when people's unbelief in the abilities of His Spirit will be changed so that they will have a powerful, living faith untainted by any self-ambition! Only then, the unity that has been impossible to attain may become possible with God (see Mark 10:27; Eph. 3:14–21; John 14:21; and Romans 12:1–2).

It is ironic that God is rejected in this world through disobedience, rebellion, and unbelief: He is the only hope for the true recovery, freedom, and victory of His Church. He is the hope of the nations, and "...all nations will come and worship before [Him]" (Revelation 15:4, NIV). His power is the only one that will break through the power of darkness, enabling us to enter the bright morning of His kingdom.

Indeed, "strait is the gate, and narrow is the way that leadeth unto life" (Matthew 7:14). Father, will You please open the door for the "morning of Your Kingdom" to come on earth and shut the door of the nightmare behind? For the One who said, "I am the narrow door" (John 10:9; Luke 13:24), and, "Surely I come quickly" (Revelation 22:12), is my only hope. Even though this earth must go through a spiritual revolution in order to be purified, I place my hope in Him for the birth of the new earth under the new heaven.

Praise be to the God and Father of our Lord Jesus Christ! In his great mercy he has given us new birth into a living hope through the resurrection of Jesus Christ from the dead, and into an inheritance that can never perish, spoil or fade—kept in heaven for you, who through faith are shielded by God's power until the coming of the salvation that is ready to be revealed in the last time. In this you greatly rejoice, though now for a little while you may have had to suffer grief in all kinds of trials. These have come so that your faith—of greater value than gold, which perishes even though refined by fire—may be proved genuine and may result in praise, glory and honor when Jesus Christ is revealed. Though you have not seen him, you love him; and even though you do not see him now, you believe in him and are filled with an inexpressible and glorious joy, for you are receiving the goal of your faith, the salvation of your souls (1 Peter 1:3-9, NIV).

I am very hopeful in Christ, for I have reached my spiritual destination—the foot of His Cross—to renew myself in Him where I first found His love for me and for the world. His Cross is the spiritual birthplace of His Church where we should be purified by repentance from man-made doctrines, Satan, and self unto God. The cross is also the gate to the Kingdom of God here on earth, as well as the Kingdom of heaven above. Both are like twin cities: one is visible and the other invisible, but both are built by the hand of God.

By the power of His cross, God willed my life back to my heavenly Father. I can now understand why I was always backtracking in the Scriptures: I have traced the truth all the way back to the Lord of creation, who caused me to recognize Him. He who created me, caused me to hunger to know Him by reading His words spoken long ago. He created a new woman in me, and so I seek to live my life as a woman of God for my Creator, through His words and the guidance of the Holy Spirit.

As I conclude my writing, peace fills my whole being as if to place the last punctuation mark in this testimony. I know I am out of Satan's "maze," placed by God in Christ Jesus as a citizen of His heavenly kingdom, among my brothers and sisters in Christ. I am now free from being held prisoner by the deception of a king frog in his small pond.

After all, it was possible to know Him in whom my father believed by faith. I made my journey back to my Father just as Jesus said, "He who receives Me will receive

Him who sent Me" (Matthew 10:40). My heavenly Father sent Jesus to look for me, lost in the confused world, just as my earthly father sent my brothers to look for me when I was late coming home from my little childhood adventure.

Satan surely meant to block my way back to my Father, intending to destroy me through my ignorance, but God desired to teach me His ways, to know Him, as He directed my path. His purposes were to raise what was made low (Luke 1:52), to bring down what was made high (Luke 3:3), to give speed to what was delayed, to make smooth and gentle what was rough, to gather what was scattered (Luke 3:17), and to bring back what was lost (Luke 19:10) for the balance and beauty to be restored in His re-creation of earth.

Father, please forgive the sins of our forefathers, even the sin of Adam and Eve, and Cain in us, as we forgive them. Please forgive our many sins of commission and omission, which are open to You before Your eyes on this earth today. We are so confused by the "good and evil" of the world-system under Satan's kingdom. Please purify us through Your Word that we may know what is the perfect will of God....and deliver us, Your children, from the darkness within and unite us as one in Christ to overcome the power of darkness together on earth.

You are the witness of the entire history of Your creation from the very beginning, including my ancestors. If You led me to write this book as I believe by faith, the end result is totally in Your hands. Therefore, if this testimony is pleasing to Your sight (according to Matthew 7:7-8), I ask in the name Jesus Christ, our Lord and Savior, for Your glory, that You may pour Your Holy Spirit upon all flesh (according to Joel 2:28-29), so that Your will may become reality on earth at last. Please restore our lives on earth as they ought to be according to Your creation-purpose. Please cause us to repent unto Christ Jesus, who died in our place to save us, so that those who died in Christ may be one with us today, according to Christ's prayer.

Please, Father, enlighten the minds of people in the dark with knowledge of the Lord of creation and the Hope of the coming kingdom of God on earth. Father, I thank you from the bottom of my heart for loving us all and making my journey back to You possible by Your grace and guidance of the "eyes."

May the love of God open our understanding and shine upon the hearts of all who place their trust in Him as their Savior and Lord, and may they experience a glorious "sunrise" of their own to share with others. May the will of Our Father be done in my life for His glory through the writing of this book, which is dedicated to Him in Christ, to His Church, and for His purpose.

Before the coming judgment of God on earth, may His harvest in the morning be great. May the fruits in response to His love be multiplied like the tender, new leaves on the bare trees in the early spring sun. May the earth be replenished with God's children under the reign of His Son, the King of the new earth, the Creator of the whole universe, for whom I sought for so long.

I thank You, Jesus, my Brother, for coming to earth in peace and speaking clearly that you "came not to condemn the world but to save it" (John 12:47), *in the language of God's love—Your Cross!*

Finally, I am at home in His rest! Praise God the Father, the Son and the Holy Spirit forever! Amen.